Silver Burdett music

George Odam
Mary Palmer
Mary Louise Reilly
Carol Rogel Scott
Authors

Darrell Bledsoe
Producer, Vocal Recordings

SIMON & SCHUSTER
EDUCATION

Contents

Music for Living 2

I'm Special (4) • A Special Person (6) • Well Done! (7) • Join In! (8) • Whistle Through the Week (8) • There's Work to Be Done (10) • On the Farm (12) • Flying a Kite (14) • A Singing Game (16) • The Story of a Gallant Ship (18) • A Tug of War (20) • A Strange Procession (22) • At the Circus (24) • Nellie Packs Her Trunk (26) • A Very Special Animal (28) • A Story Song (30) • A Familiar Story (32) • A Story from Africa (36) • The Animals Find Water (38) • Going on a Journey (40) • At the Seaside (42) • Music by the Sea (44) • Counting in Other Countries (46) • A Safety Lesson (48) • A Lullaby (50) • A Rainbow Song (52) • Counting the Stars (53) • 5-4-3-2-1-Blast Off! • What Do You Hear? Evaluations (55)

Understanding Music 58

Sounds Around Us (60) • Music Around Us (61) • A Nonsense Song (62) • Bounce and Catch (64) • Let's Pretend! (66) • A Space Adventure (67) • Fast or Slow? (68) • Racing and Resting (69) • A Musical Hand-Pat (70) • String Sounds (72) • Working with String Sounds (74) • Styles in Music (76) • A Planting Song (78) • Rise and Shine (80) • A Singing Lesson (82) • Forget Me Not! (84) • To Market, to Market (86) • A Nonsense Song (88) • Sing and Move! (90) • One Voice, Many Voices (91) • A Barnyard Scene (92) • It's Time to Dance! (94) • Sound and Silence (96) • A Silly Song (98) • The Man in the Moon (100) • Even or Uneven? (101) • *Polka* (102) • A Visitor (104) • Say It, Sing It (106) • A Lullaby (108) • Day Is Done (109) • Meow! (110) • A Song with Two Sections (112) • An Action Song (113) • Hello and Goodby (114) • A Tall Tale (116) • All Aboard! (118) • *Minuet in G* (120) • What Do You Hear? Evaluations (122)

Sharing Music 132

A Party Game (134) • An Action Song (136) • Clap and Chant (138) • From the Old West (140) • Hush! Child Sleeping (142) • Where Is the Flower? (144) • A Folk Dance (145) • Saying Goodbye (146) • A Toe-Tapping Song (148) • *Ronde* and *Saltarello* (150) • Dance a Song (152) • A Song to Sign (154) • A Quiet Time (156) • An Add-On Song (158) • Finding a Pattern (160) • Sing and Speak (162) • Rhythm Patterns to Play (163) • A Musical Scene (164) • The Snow Is Dancing (166) • A Story Song (168) • Hoot and Holler! (170) • A Surprise (172) • Wake Up! (174) • Let's Have a Parade! (170) • What Do You Hear? Evaluations (178)

Working with Sounds 180

The Sounds of the Pied Piper (182) • What the Pied Piper Did (184) • The Story of Petrouchka (186) • Going 'Like This' from China (188) • An Adventure with Alice (190) • Making an Alice Song (192) • Drums for Alice (193) • The Lobster Quadrille (194) • An African Fable (196) • Playing Drums (198) • The Animals Finish the Drum (200) • An Old Motor Car (202) • Sounds Near and Far (204) • Toad's First Car (206) • A Picture in Sound (208) • Mole Discovers a River (210) • Working with Recorded Sound (212) • Momotaro (214) • Music for a Cinema (216) • Momotaro's Journey (218) • Momotaro on His Way (220) • Momotaro Defeats the Ogres (222) • A Five-Note Melody (224) • The Story of Divali (226) • More About Divali (228) • Monkey Music (230)

Reference Bank 232

Glossary 232
Classified Index 234
Song Index 236

Acknowledgments 238
Picture Credits 238

Around, around, flew each sweet sound,
Then darted to the Sun;
Slowly the sounds came back again,
Now mix'd, now one by one.

Samuel Taylor Coleridge   from THE RIME OF
                             THE ANCIENT MARINER

MUSIC FOR LIVING

 'Tango Pasodoble' from Façade. .
.... Walton

I'm Special!

It's me!
It's something to shout about!
It's great to be nobody else
but me!

It's Me!

Words and Music by Carmino Ravosa

REFRAIN

It's me! No-bod - y else but me!

It's me! There's no one I'd rath - er be.

VERSE

1. Long or short or thin or fat,
   oh, what do I care,
   When I look in the mirror just so
   long as I'm there? *Refrain*

2. Black or white, I don't care 'bout
   the colour of my skin
   As long as I've got sump'n to keep
   my insides in. *Last Refrain*

4

LAST REFRAIN

It's me! No-bod-y else but me!

It's me! There's no one I'd rath-er be.

It's me, it's me, it's me, it's me, it's me!

Can you make up your own melody?
It should have leaps.

5

A Special Person

Why is the person in this song called Bongo Joe?

What makes him special?

bongos

maracas

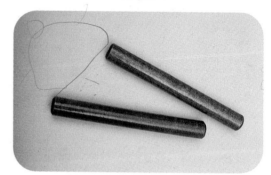

claves

Bongo Joe

Words and Music by Judy Rector Rodger

Hear the mu - sic with the bon - go beat, —

It's com - ing from the house at the end of the street,

For there lives Bon - go Joe — with his drum so grand, —

And he's the best bon - go play - er in all of the land.

Well Done!

In Italy they say 'bravo' when something is good.

They say 'bravissimo' when it is <u>very</u> good.

Bravo

Traditional British

Bra - vo! Bra - vo! Bra - vo! Bra - vis - si - mo!

Bra - vo! Bra - vo! Ver - y well done!

Bra - vo! Bra - vis - si - mo! Bra - vo! Bra - vis - si - mo!

Bra - vo! Bra - vis - si - mo! Ver - y well done!

Whistle Through the Week

Can you whistle?
Whistle after you sing
about the days of the week.

Today Is Monday

Traditional British

To-day is Mon-day, to-day is Mon-day.

(No repeat 1st time)

Mon-day's wash day. Ever-y-bod-y's hap-py?

(whistle)

You bet your life we are!

2. Tuesday's soup day . . .

3. Wednesday's roast beef . . .

4. Thursday's baked beans . . .

5. Friday's fish day . . .

6. Saturday's pay day . . .

7. Sunday's church day . . .

9

There's Work to Be Done!

Do you ever sing when you work?
Singing can help to make the task easier.

On sailing ships the sailors have to haul the ropes.
When they sing, they pull the ropes together.

Haul Away, Joe

British Sea Shanty

1. Way, haul a - way, We'll haul a - way the bow line, Way, haul a - way, oh, haul a - way, Joe.

2. Way, haul away, the packet is a-rollin', . . .

3. Louis was the King of France before the Revolution, . . .

4. Louis went a-journeying and spoilt his constitution, . . .

5. Way, haul away, We'll haul away together, . . .

6. Way, haul away, we'll haul for better weather, . . .

A hornpipe is a sailor's dance.
Does the steady beat get slower?
Does the steady beat get faster?
Does the steady beat
stay the same?

Can you hear people clapping
on this recording?

LISTENING SKILLS 1 'Hornpipe' from <u>Fantasia on British
Sea Songs</u> .... Wood

On the Farm

Here is a game you can play.
Farmers like to celebrate when the harvest is in.

Oats and Beans

English Game Song

Oats and beans and bar - ley grow,
First the far - mer sows the seed,

Oats and beans and bar - ley grow.
Then he stands and takes his ease.

Do you or I or an - y - one know
He stamps his foot and claps __ his hand,

How oats and beans and bar - ley grow?
And turns a - round to view the land!

Wait - ing for a part - ner.

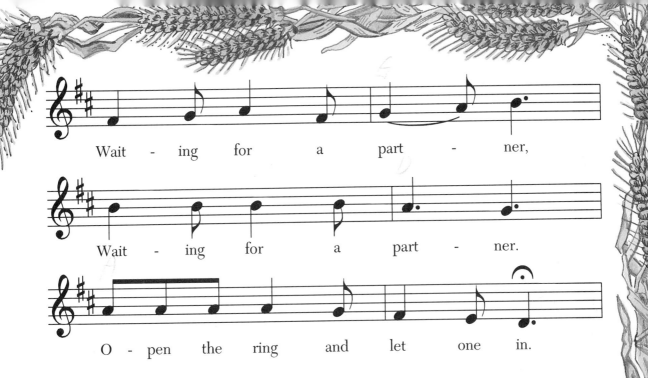

Wait - ing for a part - ner,

Wait - ing for a part - ner.

O - pen the ring and let one in.

A Now you're married you must obey,
You must be true to all you say.
You must be kind, you must be good
And both go out to chop the wood.

Flying a Kite

Can you fly a kite?
When you pull the string, the kite flies up.
When you slacken the string,
the kite comes down.

Kite Song

Words and Music by George Odam

VERSE

1. Pa - per and string and a bit of bam - boo
and the kite is there; _____
Hold - ing it stead - y, I'm mak - ing it read - y
to take the air! _____

REFRAIN

Kite, my kite on a string, let the string out,
now pull it in. Soar up, dive through the air,

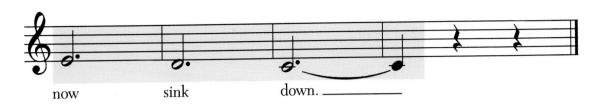

now   sink   down. _____

2. Dad's in the car and it's really not far 'til the hill's in sight.
   Ready to stop then it's up to the top where I fly my kite. *Refrain*

3. Up on the hill, now I'm standing quite still where the wind blows free.
   It's so exciting to be going kiting, just Dad and me. *Refrain*

A Singing Game

There are many churches in London.
Many have bells that ring each day.
In the old days, people heard them clearly.
Why is it harder to hear them now?

Oranges and Lemons

Traditional Song from England

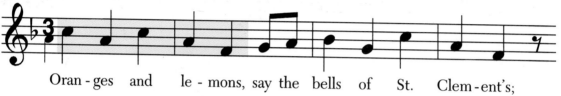

Oran - ges and le - mons, say the bells of St. Clem - ent's;

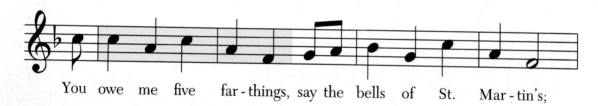

You owe me five far - things, say the bells of St. Mar - tin's;

When will you pay me? say the bells of Old Bai - ley;

When I grow rich, say the bells of Shore - ditch;

When will that be? __ say the bells of Step - ney; __

I'm sure I don't know says the great bell of Bow.

Here comes a can - dle to ___ light you to bed,

And here comes a chop - per to ___ chop off your head!

A Story of a Gallant Ship

Have you ever heard of the ship, Mary Rose?
Can you make some actions for the sinking ship?
The diver? The salvage vessel man?

The Gallant Ship

Traditional British Sea Shanty   2nd and 3rd Verse Words by George Odam

1. O, three times a-round went the gal-lant, gal-lant ship,

And three times a-round went she.

O, three times a-round went the gal-lant, gal-lant ship,

As she sank to the bot-tom of the sea,

As she sank to the bot-tom of the sea.

2. 'O, there, there she is,' says the diver with the light,
   'O, there, there she is,' says she.
   'O, there, there she is,' says the diver with the light,
   As she lies on the bottom of the sea,
   As she lies on the bottom of the sea.

18

3. 'O, pull, pull her up,' says the salvage vessel man,
'O, pull, pull her up,' says he.
'O, pull, pull her up,' says the salvage vessel man,
And she rose from the bottom of the sea,
And she rose from the bottom of the sea.

A Tug of War

This game ends with a tug of war.

Romans and British

Game Song from England

1. Have you an-y bread and wine?

For we are the Ro - mans.

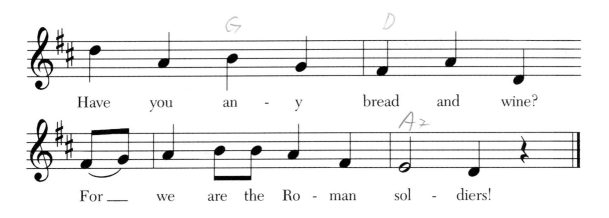

Have you an - y bread and wine?

For — we are the Ro - man sol - diers!

2. Yes, we have some bread and wine,
   For we are the British.
   Yes, we have some bread and wine,
   For we are the British soldiers.

3. Then we will have one cup full,
   For we are the Romans . . .

4. No you shan't have one cup full,
   For we are the British . . .

5. We will tell the King on you,
   For we are the Romans . . .

6. We don't care for your King or you,
   For we are the British . . .

A Strange Procession

Imagine! You are standing on a street
while these people pass by. Will it
ever finish passing by? Can you dress up
and form this strange procession?

The Court of King Caractacus

Folk Song from Britain

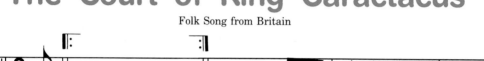

1. The court of King Ca - rac - ta-cus is just pass - ing by.

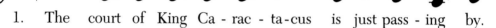

The court of King Ca - rac - ta-cus is just pass - ing by.

from FIRESIDE BOOK OF FUN AND GAME SONGS. Collected and edited by Marie Winn. © 1974 by Marie Winn and Allan Miller. Used by permission of Simon & Schuster, Inc. publishers.

The court of King Ca - rac - ta - cus is just pass - ing by.

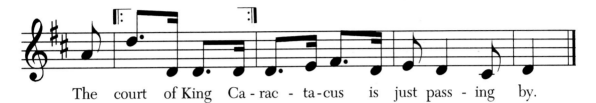

The court of King Ca - rac - ta - cus is just pass - ing by.

2. The ladies of the harem of the court of King Caractacus
   is just passing by . . .
3. The faces of the ladies of the harem . . .
4. The noses of the faces . . .
5. The powder on the noses . . .
6. The man who put the powder . . .
7. The boy who shouted 'Whiskers!' at the man . . .

At the Circus

The circus parade is beginning!
Here comes the band, leading the way.
Which circus acts are following behind?

Circus Parade

Words and Music by Milton Kaye

1. Oh, here comes the cir - cus band,

Ta - ra - ra - ra, ta - ra - ra - ra - ra,

Here comes the cir - cus band,

Ta - ra - ra - ra - ra - ra!

REFRAIN

Zing! Zing!____ Zing! Zing!____

Ta - ra - ra - ra, Ta - ra - ra - ra.

Oh, how much I love the cir - cus, Ta - ra - ra! Boom! Boom!

2. Oh, here come the elephants,
   Clump-clump-ta-ra, clump-clump-ta-ra-ra,
   Here come the elephants,
   Clump-clump-ta-ra-ra-ra. *Refrain*

3. Oh, here come the merry clowns,
   Ha-ha-ta-ra, ha-ha-ta-ra-ra,
   Here come the merry clowns,
   Ha-ha-ta-ra-ra-ra. *Refrain*

4. Oh, here come the dancing bears,
   Thump-thump-ta-ra, thump-thump-ta-ra-ra,
   Here come the dancing bears,
   Thump-thump-ta-ra-ra-ra. *Refrain*

In The Red Pony a boy dreams about a circus.
Listen to the music that the circus band plays.

 'Circus Music' from The Red Pony . . . . . Copland

BAREBACK RIDERS
W. H. BROWN

National Gallery of Art, Washington, D.C. Gift of Edgar William and Bernice Chrysler Garbisch.

25

Nellie Packs Her Trunk

Once there was an elephant who lived in India.
Her name was Nellie.
Nellie lived in a circus, but she left.
Do you think she was better off in the jungle?

Nellie the Elephant

Words by Ralph Butler   Music by Peter Hart

VERSE 1
To Bombay a travelling circus came,
They brought an intelligent elephant;
Nellie was her name.
One dark night she slipp'd her iron chain,
And off she ran to Hindustan
  and was never seen again.

REFRAIN

(A) Nellie the elephant packed her trunk
and said 'good-bye' to the circus.
Off she went with a trumpety-trump.

Trump!   Trump!   Trump!

Nellie the elephant packed her trunk
  and trundled back to the jungle.
Off she went with a trumpety-trump,

Trump!   Trump!   Trump!

B The head of the herd was calling
    far, far away.
They met one night in the silver light
    on the road to Mandalay.

(A) So, Nellie the elephant packed her trunk
    and said good-bye to the circus.
Off she went with a trumpety-trump,

Trump!   Trump!   Trump!

VERSE 2
Night by night she danced to the circus band.
When Nellie was leading the big parade
    she looked so proud and grand.
No more tricks for Nellie to perform;
They taught her how to take a bow
    when she took the crowd by storm.

REFRAIN

A Very Special Animal

This is the story
of Jackie Paper and
his friend. Jackie's friend
was a magic dragon named Puff.
What happened when Jackie Paper grew up?

Puff, the Magic Dragon

Words and Music by Peter Yarrow and Leonard Lipton

REFRAIN

Puff,   the mag - ic   drag - on   lived   by   the   sea.

And   fro - licked   in ____   the   au - tumn   mist ____

in   a   land   called   Ho - nah - lee. _____

Puff,   the mag - ic   drag - on   lived   by   the   sea.

And   fro - licked   in ____   the   au - tumn   mist ____

in   a   land   called   Ho - nah - lee.

1. Puff, the magic dragon lived by the sea,
   And frolicked in the autumn mist in a land called Honahlee.
   Little Jackie Paper loved that rascal, Puff,
   And brought him strings and sealing wax and other fancy stuff. Oh! *Refrain*

2. Together they would travel on a boat with billowed sail,
   Jackie kept a lookout perched on Puff's gigantic tail;
   Noble kings and princes would bow whene'er they came,
   Pirate ships would lower their flag when Puff roared out his name. Oh! *Refrain*

3. A dragon lives forever but not so little boys,
   Painted wings and giant rings make way for other toys;
   One grey night it happened, Jackie Paper came no more,
   And Puff, that mighty dragon he ceased his fearless roar. Oh! *Refrain*

4. His head was bent in sorrow, green scales fell like rain,
   Puff no longer went to play along the Cherry Lane;
   Without his life-long friend, Puff could not be brave,
   So, Puff, that mighty dragon, sadly slipped into his cave. Oh! *Refrain*

Puff,   the   mag   -   ic   drag   -   on

A Story Song

This song tells about Noah, an ark, and animals.

Listen for the story.

Who Built the Ark?

Black Spiritual

REFRAIN

Who built the ark?   No - ah,   No - ah,

Who built   the ark? Broth-er   No - ah built the ark.

VERSE

1. Now   did - n't old   No - ah   build   the ark? __

He   built   it   out   of   a   hick - o - ry   bark, __   2. He

2. (He) built it long, both wide and tall,
    Plenty of room for the large and small,

3. Now in come the animals two by two,
    Hippopotamus and kangaroo,

4. Now in come the animals three by three,
    Two big cats and a bumble bee. *Refrain*

5. Now in come the animals four by four,
   Two through the window and two through the door,

6. Now in come the animals five by five,
   Four little sparrows and the redbird's wife,

7. Now in come the animals six by six,
   Elephant laughed at the monkey's tricks,

8. Now in come the animals seven by seven,
   Four from home and the rest from heaven. *Refrain*

9. Now in come the animals eight by eight,
   Some were on time and the others were late,

10. Now in come the animals nine by nine,
    Some was a-shouting and some was a-crying.

11. Now in come the animals ten by ten,
    Five black roosters and five black hens,

12. Now Noah says, 'Go shut that door,
    The rain's started dropping and we can't take more.' *Refrain*

A Familiar Story

Do you remember this story?
Can you follow the story as you listen to the music?

 2 **The Three Bears**. . . . . Coates

Turn the page to find Number 11.

THE END

A Story from Africa

How the Animals Dug a Well

The earth was dry.
No rain fell.
Day after day the animals watched
the blue sky for sight of a cloud,
but no cloud appeared.

The earth grew dryer and dryer.
No rain fell.

The streams dried up.
There was little water
for small animals to drink.
The river dried up. There was little water
for big animals to drink.
Plants dried up and died for lack of water.

Still no rain fell.

So Lion, king of all the animals,
called together the chiefs of other animals.
Lion said 'We must dig a well.
Each of us must do his share to dig
a deep, deep well.
Go, chiefs, call your helpers
and your drummers.
Each in his own way must do his share
to dig a deep, deep well.'

The sound of drumming was heard
all over the land,
calling the animals of Africa.
Animals came from far and wide,
singing to the beat of the drum.

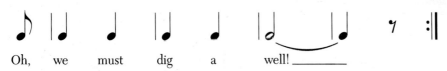

Oh,   we   must   dig   a   well! _____

36

The Jog Trot

Folk Song from Africa

I'm com - ing jog - gy jog trot! _____

I'm com - ing jog - gy jog trot! _____

I'm com - ing jog - gy jog trot! _____

Ku tu pa di, ku tu pa di, ku ___ tu pa!

The Animals Find Water

Lion greeted the animals and showed them
where to sit in a large circle.
When all was quiet, Lion called for music.
The drummer drummed.
Lion began to dance.
He danced and danced.
He kicked up the dry earth in a circle in the ground.

When Lion grew tired, he said,
'See, I have started the well.
Come, Sir Monkey,
I give my place to you. Dig!'

Sir Monkey called all his helpers.
His musicians played rattles
and scrapers. The music started.
They danced and danced.
They scratched the dry earth in Lion's tracks.

When Sir Monkey grew tired, he said,
'Come, Sir Buffalo,
I give my place to you. Dig!'

Sir Buffalo stood forth and called his helpers.
His drummer played a big, booming drum.
They danced and danced.
They tore the earth loose with their heavy feet.

The round hole grew deeper and deeper.
When Sir Buffalo grew tired, he said,
'Come, Sir Giraffe,
I give my place to you. Dig!'

Sir Giraffe stretched his long neck
and called his helpers. His drummer
made galloping sounds on the drum.
They danced and danced.
The dry earth flew in every direction.
So each animal did his share of digging
until the well became deeper and deeper.

Suddenly water gushed forth.

The animals all cried:
'The well has water!
The well has water!
Let us rejoice!
There is water to drink.'

Chum, chum, pah!

The Strength of the Lion

English Words by Ague Commari   Game Song from Tanganyika

Kou - ri - len - gay! Ka - len - gan - a   chum, chum, pah!

Kou - ri - len - gay! Ka - len - gan - a   chum, chum, pah!

Kou - ri - len - gay! Ka - len - gan - a   chum, chum, pah!

Kou - ri - len - gay! Ka - len - gan - a   chum, chum, pah!

(Sing four times)

1. Oh, the strength of the Li - on is in his tail.

2. Oh, the strength of the Monkey is in his tail.   3. . . . the Buffalo . . .

4. . . . the Giraffe . . .

from ECHOS OF AFRICA IN FOLK SONGS OF THE AMERICAS. Collected by Beatrice Landeck.

Going on a Journey

All aboard! Train is about to leave.

Same Train

Black Folk Melody   Words by Holsaert-Bailey

1. Same train — a - blow - in' at the sta - tion,

Same train, — same train. —

Same train — wait - in' for the peo - ple,

Same train, — same train. —

Same train — leav - in' the sta - tion,

Same train — be back to - mor - row,

Same train, — same train. —

From SING A SONG by Charity Bailey; © 1955 Plymouth Music Co., Inc.

40

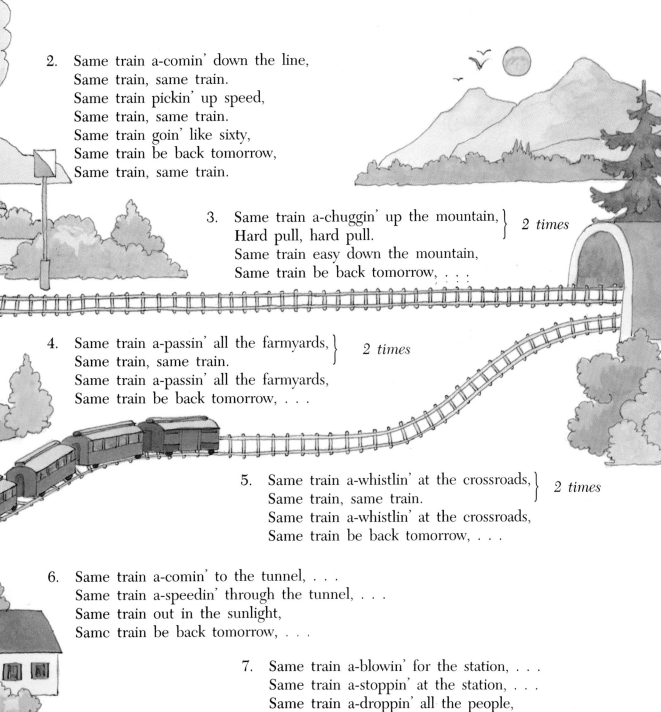

2. Same train a-comin' down the line,
   Same train, same train.
   Same train pickin' up speed,
   Same train, same train.
   Same train goin' like sixty,
   Same train be back tomorrow,
   Same train, same train.

3. Same train a-chuggin' up the mountain, ⎱ 2 times
   Hard pull, hard pull.
   Same train easy down the mountain,
   Same train be back tomorrow, . . .

4. Same train a-passin' all the farmyards, ⎱ 2 times
   Same train, same train.
   Same train a-passin' all the farmyards,
   Same train be back tomorrow, . . .

5. Same train a-whistlin' at the crossroads, ⎱ 2 times
   Same train, same train.
   Same train a-whistlin' at the crossroads,
   Same train be back tomorrow, . . .

6. Same train a-comin' to the tunnel, . . .
   Same train a-speedin' through the tunnel, . . .
   Same train out in the sunlight,
   Same train be back tomorrow, . . .

7. Same train a-blowin' for the station, . . .
   Same train a-stoppin' at the station, . . .
   Same train a-droppin' all the people,
   Same train be back tomorrow, . . .

Listen to this music about a train.
Try to picture the train in your mind.

LISTENING SKILLS 2

'The Little Train of the Caipira' from
Bachianas Brasileiras No. 2 . . . . Villa-Lobos

41

At the Seaside

Oh! I Do Like to Be Beside the Seaside

Words and Music by Lewis Ilda and John A. Glover-Kind

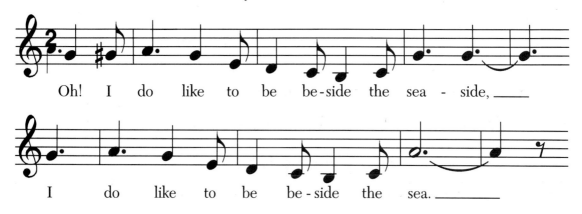

Oh! I do like to be be-side the sea - side, ____

I do like to be be-side the sea. ____

I do like to stroll up - on the prom, prom, prom,

Where the brass bands play, tid - de - ly - om - pom - pom!

So, just let me be be - side the sea - side, ____

I'll be be - side my - self with glee; _____

And there's lots of girls be - side, I should like to be be - side,

Be - side the sea - side, be - side the sea! ____

Have you ever heard a brass band?
It plays in the street. It plays in the park.
It plays by the seaside. It plays at concerts.
The musicians often wear special uniforms.
Listen to a brass band as it plays.

Fanfare and Ceremonial Prelude . . . . Langford

Music by the Sea

Here are two pieces of sea-side music.
Do you think they are very different?
The first, Tango Pasodoble, is a dance.
Many people loved to do this dance
while on holiday by the sea.

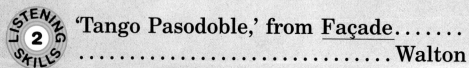

'Tango Pasodoble,' from Façade.......
.... Walton

The second piece is some music made for
Where the Wild Things Are.
Max, a small boy, goes on a fantastic journey.
He sails his boat to the island
where the wild things are.
On the way he meets a sea-monster!

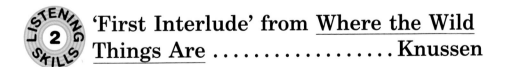 'First Interlude' from Where the Wild
Things Are ....Knussen

Can you make a picture in sound of a boat trip?
What sounds might you use?
Will your music be for instruments or voices?

Counting in Other Countries

What words do you use to count from one to ten?

Children in other lands use other words. Listen for their counting words in this song.

Counting Song

Children's Song from Mexico   Verse 1 Words by Lucille Wood
Verses 2 and 3 Words by George Odam

Spanish

1. U - no, dos, y tres,   Cua - tro, cin - co, seis;

Sie - te, o - cho, nue - ve,   I can count to diez.

REFRAIN

La la la la la, La la la la la, La la la la la la;

La la la la la, La la la la la, La la la la la la.

French

2. Une, deux, et trois,

   Quatre, cinque, six,

   Sept, et huit, et neuf

   I can count to dix.

   La la la la la . . .

German

3. Eins, und zwei, und drei,

   Vier, und fünf, und sechs,

   Sieben, acht, und neun,

   I can count to zehn.

   La la la la la . . .

Have you visited another country?
Did the children who live there speak

Spanish?   French?   German?

Perhaps they even spoke different languages?
Do you remember what they were?

A Safety Lesson

The boy and girl in this song live in Trinidad. They sing about the same things you do.

Their mother teaches them how to keep safe. What does she tell them to do?

Growing-Up Song

Calypso from Trinidad

REFRAIN

I am a lit-tle boy / girl from Tri-ni-dad, ___

Some-times I am good, some-times I am bad.

Ma-ma she talk, talk all the day ___

48

How   I   should grow up   and how   **C**   I   should play.

VERSE

Keep out   of   fire, ___   you   will   get   burned, ___

Keep out   of   fire, ___   you   will   get   burned; ___

I don't   be - lieve her, ___   try   to   de - ceive her, ___

No   more   play with   fire ___   **C**   I   have   learned.

A Lullaby

This song comes from India.
It is a lullaby.
Do you know what a lullaby is?
A lullaby is a song to sing a baby to sleep.
Do you have a baby brother or baby sister?
Perhaps you could sing this song to the baby.

Khasi's Lullaby

Folk Song from India

Ha - ri cu - cu, Ya - ri cu - cu, ___

Ha - ri cu - cu ___ e - le;

Ha - ri cu - cu, Ya - ri cu - cu, ___

Ya - ri cu - cu ___ e - le.

Ha - ri cu - cu, Ya - ri cu - cu,

from THIRTY FOLK SONGS. Used by permission William Elkin Music Services.

Ha - ri cu - cu _____ e - le;

Ha - ri cu - cu, Ya - ri cu - cu,

Ya - ri cu - cu _____ e - le.

Lullaby, Oh, Lullaby!

Lullaby, oh, lullaby!
Flowers are closed and lambs are sleeping;
Lullaby, oh, lullaby!
Stars are up, the moon is peeping;
Lullaby, oh, lullaby!
While the birds are silence keeping,
(Lullaby, oh, lullaby!)
Sleep, my baby, fall a-sleeping,
Lullaby, oh, lullaby!

Christina Rossetti

A Rainbow Song

Can you shut your eyes and think about a colour? Can you shut your eyes and think about a sound?

Sing a Rainbow

Words and Music by Arthur Hamilton

REFRAIN

Red and yel - low and pink and green,

Pur - ple and or - ange and blue,

I can sing a rain - bow, sing a rain - bow,

sing a rain - bow too. _____

Fine

Listen with your eyes.
Listen with your eyes
And sing everything you see

You can sing a rainbow,
Sing a rainbow,
Sing along with me. *Da Capo al Fine*

Counting the Stars

Twinkle, twinkle, little star,
How I wonder what you are!

Have you ever seen the night sky
filled with twinkling stars?
Did it make you wonder?
Did it make you dream?

Star Song

Folk Song from Austria

I count-ed in the heav-en, Where the moon shed its light,

White stars that num-bered sev-en, They were twin-kling so bright.

REFRAIN

I count-ed one, I count-ed two, I count-ed three,

I count-ed four, I count-ed five, I count-ed six,

I count-ed sev'n, Good night.

5-4-3-2-1-Blast Off!

Do you ever wonder what space is like?
Do you ever dream about walking
on the moon?

The child in this song does.

Mission Control

Words and Music by Carmino Ravosa

Mis-sion Con-trol, __ do you read me?

Will you please save __ me a place?

Mis-sion Con-trol, __ do you need me

On the next rock-et in space?

1. May-be I'm small, __ but I'm grow-ing.

Watch, and one day __ you will see.

Space is wide o - pen and wait - ing for me. _____

So, Mis - sion Con - trol, __ do you read me?

I real - ly don't take __ too much room.

Mis - sion Con - trol, __ do you need me

Last time, to Ending

On the next trip to the moon?

2. I want to study the planets.
   I want to study the stars.
   I want to go up to Venus, or Mars.
   So, Mission Control . . .

3. I'm working hard, and I'm certain
   An astronaut's what I will be.
   The sky is the limit for someone like me.
   So, Mission Control . . .

Ending (spoken):
   Mission Control, do you read me?
   I'll be seeing you in about twenty years.
   Until then, over and out.

What Do You Hear 1

Upwards and Downwards

You will hear four songs. As each number is called, listen to the song and decide how the music moves.

Do the notes move mostly downwards?

Do the notes move mostly upwards?

On your answer sheet, circle the arrow that shows your answer.

1. Oats and Beans

2. The Very Best Band

3. Kite Song

4. Simple and Easy

What Do You Hear 2

Fast and Slow

Some songs you have sung are fast and lively. Others are slower and gentler. As each number is called you will hear a song from your book. Decide if the song is fast or slow. Circle your answers.

1. Khasi's Lullaby   Fast   Slow

2. Circus Parade   Fast   Slow

3. Mission Control   Fast   Slow

4. Star Song   Fast   Slow

5. Oh! I Do Like to Be Beside the Seaside   Fast   Slow

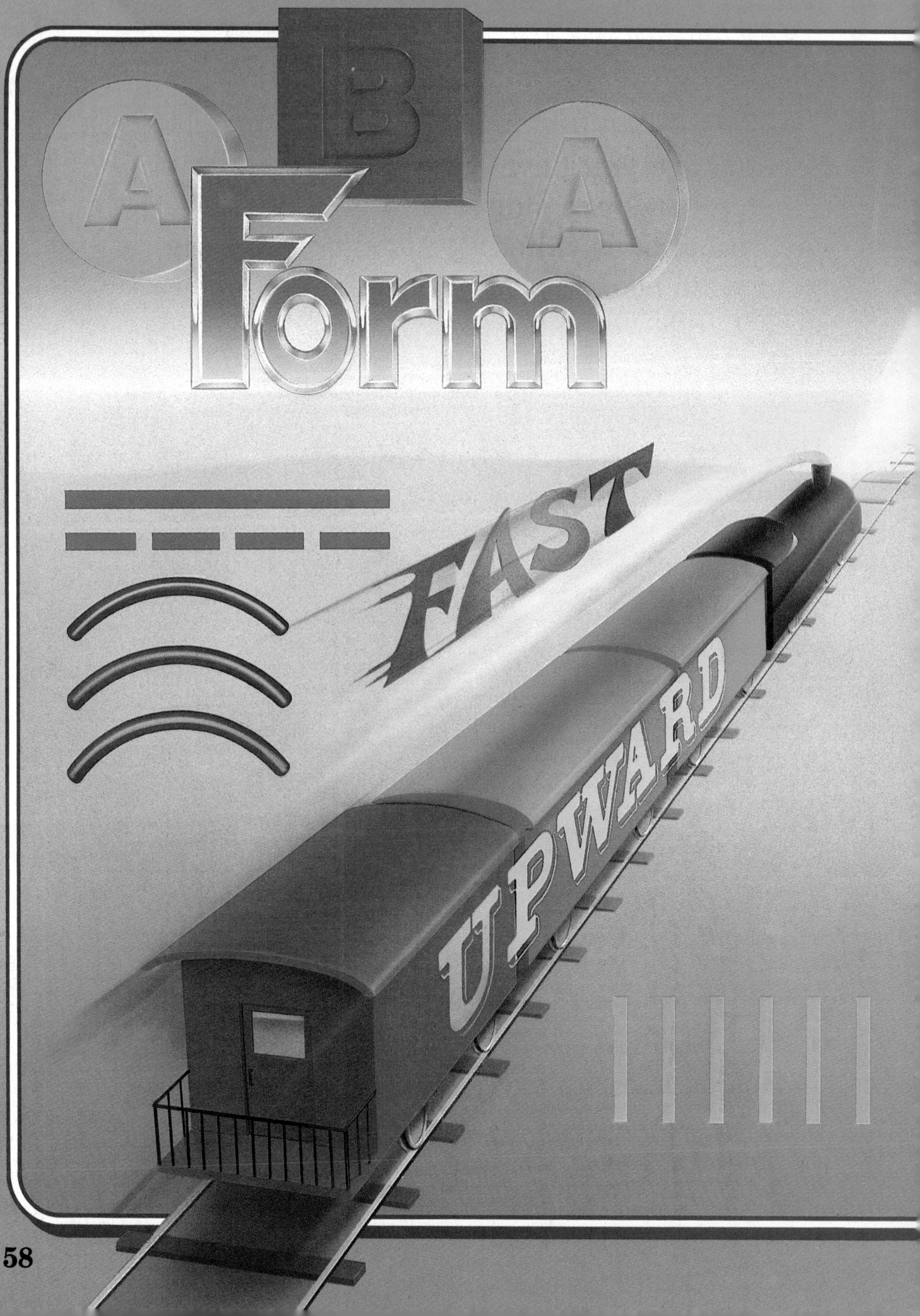
A
B
A
Form
FAST
UPWARD

Sounds Around Us

Look at the pictures.

Imagine that they can make sounds.
Describe the sounds you 'hear.'
Use the words below to help you.

high	low	fast	slow
loud	soft	long	short

Music Around Us

Listen to the music on the recording.

Point to the word that matches the sounds
you hear.

high   low
loud   soft

fast   slow
long   short

A Nonsense Song

Listen for the nonsense words in this song.

Waddaly Atcha

Words and Music by Kassel-Stitzel

Wad - da - ly a - tcha, wad - da - ly a - tcha,

Doo - dle - ee - doo, _ doo - dle - ee - doo; _

Wad - da - ly a - tcha, wad - da - ly a - tcha,

Doo - dle - ee - doo, _ doo - dle - ee - doo. _

It's the sim - pl - est thing, _ noth - in' much to ___ it, ___

All you got to do is doo - dle - ee - doo it; ___

I like the rest, — But the part I love best, —

It goes doo-dle-ee, doo-dle-ee-doo. Whoo!

You can do a hand-jive with 'Waddaly Atcha.'
Here are the actions.

Bounce and Catch

Listen to this song.
Can you feel the steady beat?

Show the beat by bouncing and
catching a ball.

One, Two, Three, Alary

Playground Chant

1. One, two, three, a - lar - y,

My first name is Mar - y.

If you think it nec - es - sar - y,

Look it up in the dic - tion - ar - y.

2. One, two, three, alary,
   I saw Peter Terry
   Sitting on a bumbleberry,
   Eating lots of delicious
   cherries.

3. One, two, three, alary,
   Lost my new canary.
   When you find him,
   call him Barry.
   One, two, three, alary.

From *Sally Go Round the Sun* by Edith Fowke. Reprinted by permission of the author.

Play this chime bar part to accompany the song.

Listen to this music.
It gives the feeling of a ball in motion.
Try to picture the ball in your mind.
Can you see how it moves?

'The Ball' from <u>Children's Games</u> . . . . . Bizet

Let's Pretend!

Children in Japan tell about a rabbit who lives in the moon.

This rabbit pounds rice into cakes for the New Year's celebration.

The rabbit in this song lives on the earth. He seems to wish he were the rabbit in the moon.

Rabbit

Folk Song from Japan

Oh, Rab - bit, jump - ing free,

Tell me, Rab - bit, what you see.

'When I look up in - to the sky, ___

Moon is there; here ___ am I.' _____

Try playing steady beats on a woodblock.
Follow these notes as you play.

A Space Adventure

Imagine that you are an astronaut in
your big space suit.
Your spacecraft has just landed
on the moon.

 Now listen to the recording.
Moon Music . . . . L. Williams

When you hear a steady beat,
pretend to walk on the moon.

When you hear no beat,
pretend to float in space.

Fast or Slow?

How would you move climbing up a
mountain—fast or slow?
How would you move coming down a
mountain? Going around a mountain?

We're Going Round the Mountain

Folk Song from Mississippi

1. We're go - ing round the moun - tain, two by two,

We're go - ing round the moun - tain, two by two,

We're go - ing round the moun - tain, two by two,

So rise, Sal - ly, rise.

2. Let me see you make an
   action, two by two, . . .

3. That's a very fine
   action, two by two, . . .

Play steady beats on
chime bars while
others sing.

68

Racing and Resting

Look at the song title.
Does it suggest fast singing or slow singing?

Race You down the Mountain

Words and Music by Woody Guthrie and Marjorie Mazia

1. I'll race you down the moun-tain,

I'll race you down the moun-tain,

I'll race you down the moun-tain,

We'll see who gets there first.

2. Let's run and jump the river, (3 times)
   We'll see who gets there first.

3. I hear myself a-huffin',
   A-huffin' and a-puffin',
   I hear myself a-huffin',
   We'll see who gets there first.

4. We'll rest beside the water, (3 times)
   We'll see who gets there first.

69

A Musical Hand-Pat

Children in Africa do a hand-pat with this song.

Try to learn the actions from the pictures.

Kee-Chee

Game from Zaire

Ah wu - ne ku - ne cha o wu - ni,

Ah wu - ne ku - ne cha o wu - ni;

Ah yi yi yi - ki ay kae ay - na,

Ah yi yi yi - ki ay kae ay - na;

A oo_____ ah dee mee kee - chee.

1.

2.

3.

4.

String Sounds

String instruments make many
different sounds.

Listen.
Then describe the sounds that you hear.

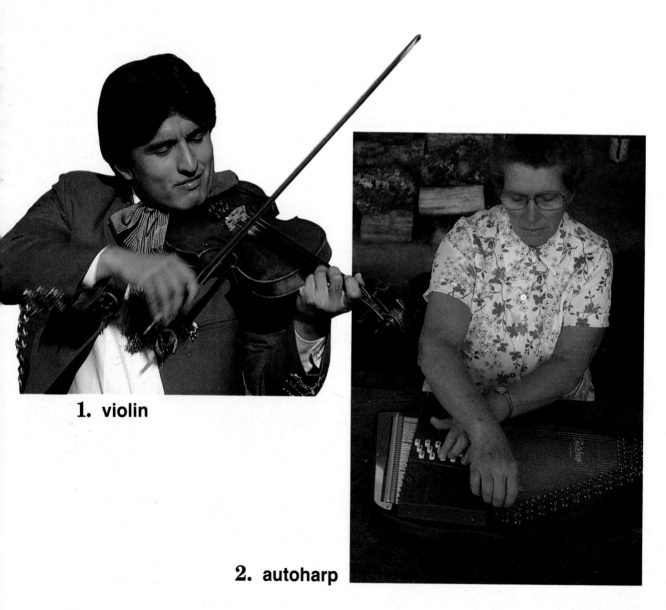

1. **violin**

2. **autoharp**

3. koto

4. musical bow

5. dulcimer

Working with String Sounds

Pluck a rubber band.
How does it sound?

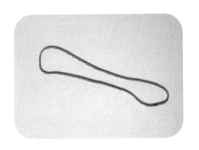

Try to make the sound louder.
Here is one idea.

Can you think of another way
to make the sound louder?

Here is a string instrument that you
can make. It is called a <u>diddley bow</u>.

Try to play the
diddley bow as
shown here.

Listen to the sound of a diddley bow on
the recording.

 Diddley Bow Music

75

Styles in Music

Keep the beat by
pretending to play
a guitar.

Rock About My Saro Jane

American Folk Song

Oh,   rock a-bout   my   Sa - ro ___   Jane, ___

Oh,   rock a-bout   my   Sa - ro   Jane, ___

Oh, there's noth-ing   to   do   but   sit down   and   sing

And   rock a-bout   my   Sa - ro   Jane. ___

A Planting Song

This song tells of a place where the soil is sandy.
What crop do the people grow there?

Sandy Land

Folk Song from Oklahoma

1. Make my liv-in' in sand-y land,

Make my liv-in' in sand-y land,

Make my liv-in' in sand-y land,

La - dies, fare you well.

2. Raise sweet potatoes in sandy land, (*3 times*)
   Ladies, fare you well.

3. Dig sweet potatoes in sandy land, (*3 times*)
   Ladies, fare you well.

Play an introduction when the class sings
the song.
Follow these notes.

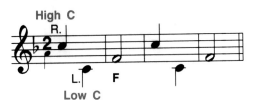

Rise and Shine

Children in France sing about bells that ring in the morning. These bells help to wake up the town.

Do the bells wake up everyone? Listen to find out.

Are You Sleeping?

Folk Song from France

Are you sleep - ing, Are you sleep - ing,

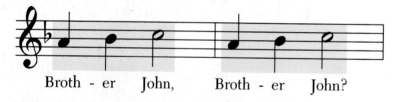

Broth - er John, Broth - er John?

Morn - ing bells are ring - ing, Morn - ing bells are ring - ing,

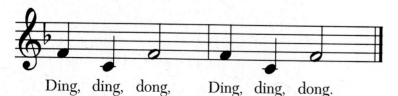

Ding, ding, dong, Ding, ding, dong.

Play one of these chime bar
parts to accompany the
song.

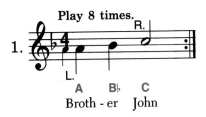

1.

Play 8 times.

R.

L.

A   B♭   C

Broth - er   John

2.

Play 8 times.

R.

L.

F   C   F

Ding ding dong

Listen to this music.

Pretend that you are
a bell ringer.
Show how you would
move to make the
bells ring.

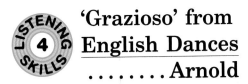

LISTENING SKILLS 4

'Grazioso' from
English Dances
. . . . Arnold

A Singing Lesson

What do you begin with when you read?
What do you begin with when you sing?

Listen to this song for the answers.

Do-Re-Mi

From THE SOUND OF MUSIC
Music by Richard Rodgers   Words by Oscar Hammerstein II

The first three notes just hap-pen to be

Chorus

Do - re - mi! Do - re - mi!

Solo

Do - re - mi - fa - so - la - ti

B REFRAIN

All

<u>Doe</u> — a deer, a female deer,
Low C

<u>Ray</u> — a drop of golden sun,
D

<u>Me</u> — a name I call myself,
E

<u>Far</u> — a long, long way to run.
F

<u>Sew</u> — a needle pulling thread,
G

<u>La</u> — a note to follow sew,
A

<u>Tea</u> — a drink with jam and bread
B

That will bring us back to doe!
  (Repeat refrain.)   **High C**

DO - RE - MI - FA - SO - LA - TI - DO!

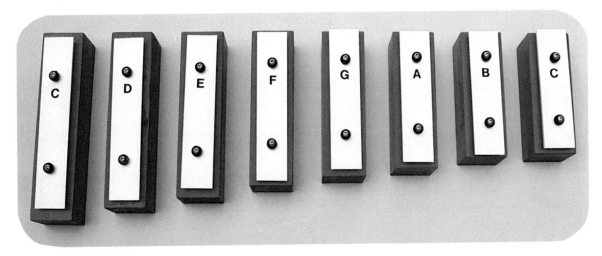

Forget Me Not!

You know that notes can repeat.

— — — — —

Repeated notes can also move by step.

— — — — —

Try to hear notes repeating and stepping in this song.

Rocky Mountain

VERSE

Southern Folk Song

1. Rock - y moun - tain, rock - y moun - tain,

Rock - y moun - tain high;

When you're on that rock - y moun - tain,

Hang your head and cry!

REFRAIN

Do,   do,   do,   do,
Do   re - mem - ber   me;
Do,   do,   do,   do,
A   G   F
Do   re - mem - ber   me.

2. Sunny valley, sunny valley,
   Sunny valley low;
   When you're in that
      sunny valley,
   Sing it soft and slow.
   Refrain

3. Stormy ocean, stormy ocean,
   Stormy ocean wide;
   When you're on that deep
      blue sea,
   There's no place you can hide.
   Refrain

Play this part as an introduction to
'Rocky Mountain.'
Then play it over and over to accompany
the song.
Do the notes repeat? Step? Leap?

To Market, to Market!

You know that notes can
repeat. — — — — —

You know that notes can leap. —   —

                                    — —

Some groups of notes move both ways.
They repeat and also leap.

— — —   — —

    — —   —

There Was a Little Woman

Folk Song from England

There was a lit-tle wom-an,   As I've heard tell,

Fol,   lol,   did-dle, did-dle, dol;

She — went to mar-ket,   Some eggs for to sell,

Fol,   lol,   did-dle, did-dle, dol;

High C   **Low C**

She   went   to   mar - ket   all   on   a   mar - ket   day,

And   she   fell   a - sleep   up - on   the   King's ___   High - way;

Fol   de   rol   de   lol   lol,   lol   lol   lol,

Fol,   lol,   did - dle,   did - dle,   dol.

A Nonsense Song

Find the steps, leaps,
and repeated notes
in this song.

Chumbara

French-Canadian Folk Song

1. Chum - ba - ra, _____ chum - ba - ra,

Chum - ba - ra, _____ chum - ba - ra,

Chum - ba - ra, _____ chum - ba - ra,

Chum, chum, chum, chum, chum, chum, chum, chum,

Chum - ba - ra, _____ chum - ba - ra,

Chum - ba - ra, _____ chum - ba - ra,

Chum - ba - ra, _____ chum - ba - ra, chum, chum!

2. Fy-do-lee 3. Chow-ber-ski

Sing and Move!

Some phrases in this song say 'Dum-a-la-lum.'
Which 'Dum-a-la-lum' phrase begins lower
than the others?
Which one has notes that keep leaping
downward?

Shake Hands, Mary

Black American Children's Song

1. Shake hands, Mar - y,   Dum - a - la - lum. _

Shake hands, Mar - y,   Dum - a - la - lum. _

REFRAIN

Lum, lum, lum, lum,   Dum - a - la - lum. _

Lum, lum, lum, lum,   Dum - a - la - lum. _

2. Strut, Mary,
    Dum-a-la-lum.
    Strut, Mary,
    Dum-a-la-lum. *Refrain*

3. Dance, Mary,
    Dum-a-la-lum.
    Dance, Mary,
    Dum-a-la-lum. *Refrain*

From PLAY SONGS OF THE DEEP SOUTH by Altona Trent-Johns. Copyright by Association for the Study of Afro-American Life and History, Inc. Used by permission.

90

One Voice, Many Voices

Listen to the recording.
Is the whole song sung by one voice?
Is it all sung by a group of voices?
Tell what you hear on the recording.

Michael, Row the Boat Ashore

Black-American Work Song

Solo

1. Mich - ael,   row   the boat a - shore,

Chorus

Hal - le - lu - jah!

Solo

Mich - ael,   row   the boat a - shore,

Chorus

Hal - le - lu - jah!

2. Noah was a gentle man, . . .

3. Gabriel, blow the trumpet strong, . . .

4. Brother, help me turn the wheel, . . .

A Barnyard Scene

It is a sunny day.
Big brown dog is far away.
So chickens, ducklings, and geese come out
to play.

In the Barnyard

Music by Milton Kaye   Words by Dorothy Aldis

In — the barn - yard   chick - ens   walk,

They   jerk — their   heads — and   peck — and   talk

While   yel - low   duck-lings   run   a - round

Like   but - ter - balls   up - on   the   ground.

And   some   geese,   tre - men - dous   proud,

Point   their   nos - es   at   a   cloud. _____

The crotchets below show how the chickens
move in this song.
Find the crotchets.

Which notes show the shorter movements of
the ducklings?

Which notes show the longer movements of
the geese?

Quavers:

Crotchets:

Minims:

Move to the short sounds and longer
sounds in this music.

'Ballet of the Unhatched Chicks' from
Pictures at an Exhibition........Mussorgsky

It's Time to Dance!

Long ago there was no TV or radio.
People made their own entertainment.
They sang, danced, and played instruments.

Clear the Kitchen

As Sung in Pennsylvania by Emma Katurah Grenoble

Down in Vir - gin - ia one af - ter - noon,

We swept the floor with a brand new broom;

And then we all would form a ring,

And this is the song that we would sing: ___

REFRAIN

'Clear the kitch - en, young folks, old folks,

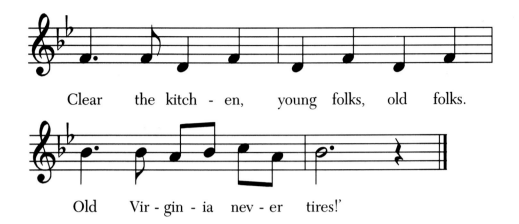

Clear the kitch - en, young folks, old folks.

Old Vir - gin - ia nev - er tires!'

Play patterns of long and short sounds with this song.

Dancing feet:

Clear the kitch - en, clear the kitch - en!

Repeat over and over.

Steady beat:

Young folks, old folks

Repeat over and over.

Broom:

Swish, swish

Repeat over and over.

HOME SWEET HOME

Sound and Silence

Listen for Mister Sun's name
in this song.

Mister Sun

Traditional

Oh, Mis - ter Sun,   Sun,   Mis - ter Gold-en Sun,

Please shine down on   me.

Oh, Mis - ter Sun,   Sun,   Mis - ter Gold-en Sun,

Hid - ing be - hind a   tree.

These lit - tle chil - dren are ____ ask - ing you

To please come out so we can play with you.

Oh, Mis-ter Sun, Sun, Mis-ter Gold-en Sun,

Please shine down on me. _____

This Happy Day

Every morning when the sun
Comes smiling up on everyone,
It's lots of fun
To say good morning to the sun.
    Good morning, Sun!

Every evening after play
When the sunshine goes away,
It's nice to say,
Thank you for this happy day,
    This happy day!

Harry Behn

A Silly Song

Read the title of this song aloud.

How many sounds or syllables does each word have?

Listen for the sound of Polly Wolly Doodle in the song.

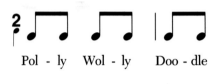

Polly Wolly Doodle

American Folk Song

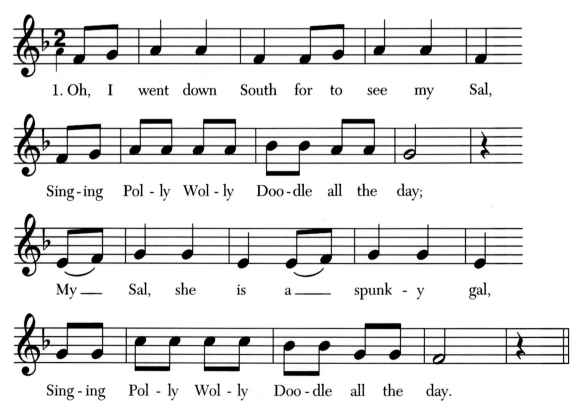

1. Oh, I went down South for to see my Sal,

Sing-ing Pol-ly Wol-ly Doo-dle all the day;

My — Sal, she is a — spunk-y gal,

Sing-ing Pol-ly Wol-ly Doo-dle all the day.

REFRAIN

Fare thee well, _____ fare thee well, _____

Fare thee well, my fair - y fay, _____

For I'm goin' to Lou' - si - an - a,

For to see my Su - sy - an - na,

Sing-ing Pol - ly Wol - ly Doo-dle all the day. _____

2. Oh, my Sal, she is a maiden fair,
   Singing Polly Wolly Doodle all the day;
   With curly eyes and laughing hair,
   Singing Polly Wolly Doodle all the day.
   Refrain

3. Behind the barn, down on my knees, . . .
   I thought I heard a chicken sneeze, . . .

4. He sneezed so hard with the whooping cough, . . .
   He sneezed his head and tail right off, . . .

The Man in the Moon

There was a man lived in the moon.
What was his name?

Aiken Drum

Folk Song from Scotland

1. There was a man lived in the moon,
Lived in the moon, lived in the moon,
There was a man lived in the moon,
And his name was Ai-ken Drum.

2. And his hat was made of good cream cheese, . . .
And his name was Aiken Drum.

3. And his coat was made of good roast beef, . . .

4. And his buttons were made of raisins, . . .

5. And he played upon a ladle, . . .

Play the sound of Aiken Drum's name—

Ai - ken Drum

100

Even or Uneven?

Listen for the name <u>Lazy John</u> in this song.
Clap the rhythm pattern when you hear it.

La - zy John

Lazy John

Words and Music by Alan Lomax and Jean Ritchie

1. La - zy John, La - zy John, Tell me where you've been.

Just got back from La - zy Town,

I'm go - in' back a - gain.

REFRAIN

O - ho, ba - by, o - ho, O - ho, ba - by, o - ho;

O - ho, ba - by, o - ho, I'm go - in' back a - gain.

2. Lazy John, Lazy John,
Tell me what you do.
Sit beside a hollow tree
And dream the whole day through.
Oho, baby, oho, *(3 times)*
And dream the whole day through.

Polka

Follow the score below as you listen to the music.
The numbers called on the recording will help you.

 'Polka' from <u>The Golden Age</u> . . .
. . . . <u>Shostakovich</u>

1. **Introduction**

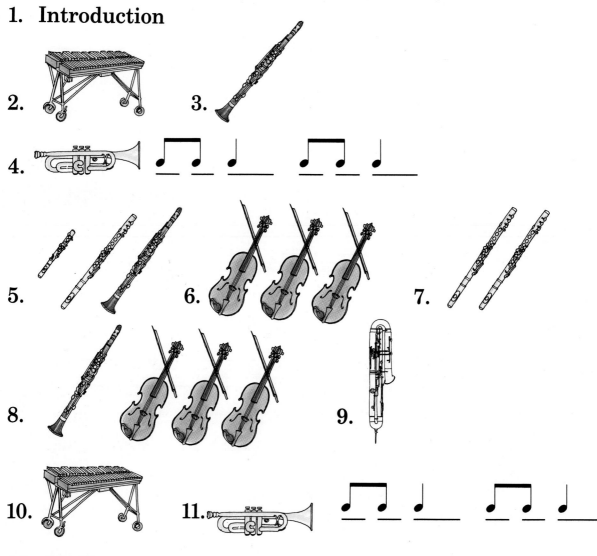

12. **Ending**

This instrument is a trombone.

Did you hear its sliding sounds in 'Polka'?
The trombone acts like a clown in this music.
It has no melody of its own to play.
Instead, it interrupts the other instruments.

Listen to 'Polka' again.
Follow the score on page 102.
Listen for the instruments at number 5 in
the score.
Can you hear the trombone interrupting them?

Try to hear which other instruments the
trombone interrupts.

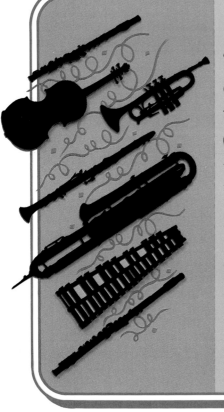

About the Music

'Polka' is a piece from a ballet called The Golden Age. It was written by Dmitri Shostakovich (dih MEE tree shoh stah KOH vihtch). 'Polka' is an example of humour in music. It is a kind of musical joke. The piece is full of short, happy-sounding melodies. What a good time Shostakovich must have had writing it. And what fun musicians have playing it!

A Visitor

Listen for the things that the Butzemann
does in this song.

The Butzemann

Folk Melody from Germany   Words by Trudi Eichenlaub

There   is   a   lit - tle   But - ze - mann

Who   danc - es   round   our   house   at   night,

There   is   a   lit - tle   But - ze - mann

Who   danc - es   round   our   house.

104

He shakes like this and shakes like that,

Then flings his sack be - hind his back,

There is a lit - tle But - ze - mann

Who danc - es round our house.

Say It, Sing It.

We speak in phrases when we recite a poem.

Who Has Seen the Wind?

Who has seen the wind?
  Neither I nor you:
But when the leaves hang trembling
  The wind is passing thro'.

Who has seen the wind?
  Neither you nor I:
But when the trees bow down their heads
  The wind is passing by.

Christina Rossetti

We sing phrases in a song.

Who Has Seen the Wind?

Melody from *Zion's Harp*   Words by Christina Rossetti

1. Who has seen the wind? ____

Nei - ther I nor ___ you!

But when the leaves hang trem - bling

From SING FOR JOY edited and compiled by Norman and Margaret Mealy. © 1961 by the Seabury Press, Inc.

The wind is pass-ing thro',

The wind is pass-ing — thro'.

2. Who has seen the wind?
   Neither you nor I:
   But when the trees bow
     down their heads
   The wind is passing by,
   The wind is passing by.

Try moving to the phrases in this music.

LISTENING SKILLS 4 'The Swan' from Carnival of the Animals.............Saint-Saëns

A Lullaby

Find the phrases in this song.

At the Gate of Heav'n

Basque Folk Song

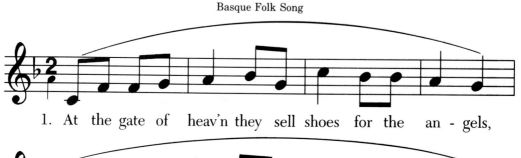

1. At the gate of heav'n they sell shoes for the an - gels,

Lit - tle bare-foot an - gels, oh, come now and buy them.

Sleep, my ___ ba - by, Sleep, O my ba - by,

Sleep, ___ O my ba - by, a - rru, a - rru.

2. God will send his blessing to
    all babes a-sleeping,
    God will help the mothers as
    watch they are keeping.
    Sleep, my baby,
    Sleep, O my baby,
    Sleep, O my baby, arru, arru.

How many long phrases did you sing?
How many short phrases did you sing?

Day Is Done

Try swaying to this music.
Face a different part of the room for
each phrase.

Ninna-nanna

Folk Song from Italy   English Words by Ann Scibilia

Nin - na - nan - na,   'Lul - la - by,' sings the moth - er;
Nin - na - nan - na,   còc - co - lo del - la mam - ma;

Nin - na - nan - na,   'Lul - la - by, Lit - tle One.' __
Nin - na - nan - na,   còc - co - lo del __ pap - pa, ___

Nin - na - nan - na,   'Lul - la - by,' sings the fa - ther;
Nin - na - nan - na,   còc - co - lo del - la mam - ma;

Nin - na - nan - na,   'Lul - la - by, day is done.'
Nin - na - nan - na,   còc - co - lo del pap - pa.

Ninna-nanna, còccolo della mamma;
Ninna-nanna, còccolo del pappa.   } *2 times*

109

Miaouw!

This song tells about a tomcat.
Listen for the story.

The Cat

Folk Melody from Brazil   Words by Verne Muñoz

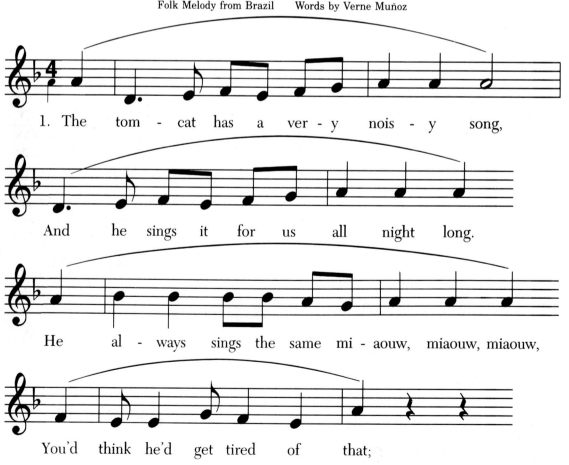

1. The tom - cat has a ver - y nois - y song,

And he sings it for us all night long.

He al - ways sings the same mi - aouw, miaouw, miaouw,

You'd think he'd get tired of that;

He al-ways sings the same mi-aouw, miaouw, miaouw,

(Spoken)

You'd think he'd get tired of that. Mi-aouw! Scat!

2. I opened up the door and chased the cat;
Tomcat ran, that was the end of that!
But soon I heard that old miaouw,
   miaouw, miaouw,   } *2 times*
I knew that the cat was back.
Miaouw! Scat!

Listen for the sound of two cats in this music.

LISTENING SKILLS 4 'Love for Two Cats' from L'Enfant et les sortilèges . . . . Ravel

A Song with Two Sections

Keep time with the steady beat.
Pat your lap during section A.
Clap your hands during section B.

Built My Lady a Fine Brick House

Folk Song from Texas

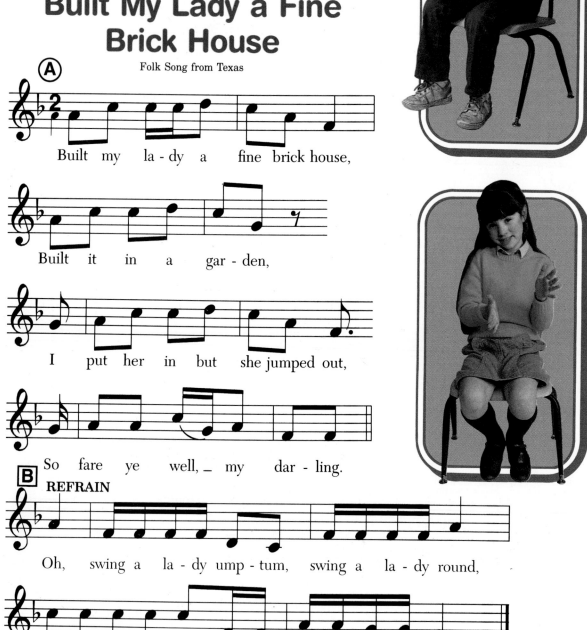

Built my la - dy a fine brick house,

Built it in a gar - den,

I put her in but she jumped out,

So fare ye well, — my dar - ling.

B REFRAIN

Oh, swing a la - dy ump - tum, swing a la - dy round,

Swing a la - dy ump - tum and prom - e - nade a - round.

An Action Song

Act out the words as you sing this song.

Scrapin' Up Sand

American Folk Song

A

1. Scrap-in' up the sand from the bot-tom of the sea,

Shi - loh!   Shi - loh!

Scrap-in' up the sand from the bot-tom of the sea,

Shi - loh! Li - za Jane!

B REFRAIN

Oh, how I'll miss you! Oh, what a shame!

Oh, how I'll miss you!   Bye, bye, Li - za Jane!

F♯   E   D

2. Pickin' up the pears that have
   fallen from the tree, . . .

3. Pickin' out the weeds from the
   watermelon patch, . . .

Hello and Good-by

Show that you hear two sections
in this song.

Move when you hear section A.
Stop and sing when you hear section B.

Come and Dance

American Folk Song   Words Adapted

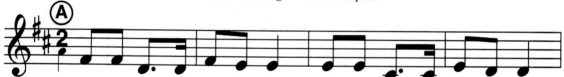

1. Come a-long and dance with me, Come a-long and dance with me,

Come a-long and dance with me, Love-ly Su-sie Brown.

Fare thee well, my charm-ing girl, Fare thee well, I'm gone;

Fare thee well, my charm-ing girl, With gold-en slip-pers on.

2. Round the circle we will go,
   Round the circle we will go,
   Round the circle we will go,
   Lovely Susie Brown. *Refrain*

From *The American Songbag*, Carl Sandburg—compiler; Harcourt Brace Jovanovich, Inc.—publisher

A Tall Tale

These drawings show the two sections in 'Old Dan Tucker.'

Do you think the sections will sound the same or different?
Why?

Old Dan Tucker

American Folk Song

1. Old Dan Tuck-er was a might-y man,

He washed his face in the fry - ing pan,

Combed his hair with a wag - on wheel,

Had a tooth - ache in his heel;

B REFRAIN

So get out the way, Old Dan Tuck - er;

Get out the way, Old Dan Tuck - er;

Get out the way, Old Dan Tuck - er,

You're too late to get your sup - per.

2. Old Dan Tucker came to town,
    Riding a billy goat, leading a hound;
    Hound dog barked, then billy goat jumped;
    Dan fell off and landed on a stump; *Refrain*

SHERIFF POST OFFICE

117

All Aboard!

Listen to this song. It has two different sections, A and B. Which section does it end with?   Which pattern below shows the form of the song?

1.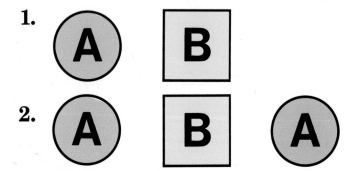

2.

Get on Board

Black Spiritual

(A) Get on board, lit - tle chil - dren,

Get on board, lit - tle chil - dren,

Get on board, lit - tle chil - dren,

There's room for man - y - a more.

118

Minuet in G

A minuet is a stately dance in ABA form.

You can dance with the recording.
Move with a partner during section A.
Move by yourself during section B.

The pictures below show how to move for
each section.

 Minuet in G . . . . **Beethoven**

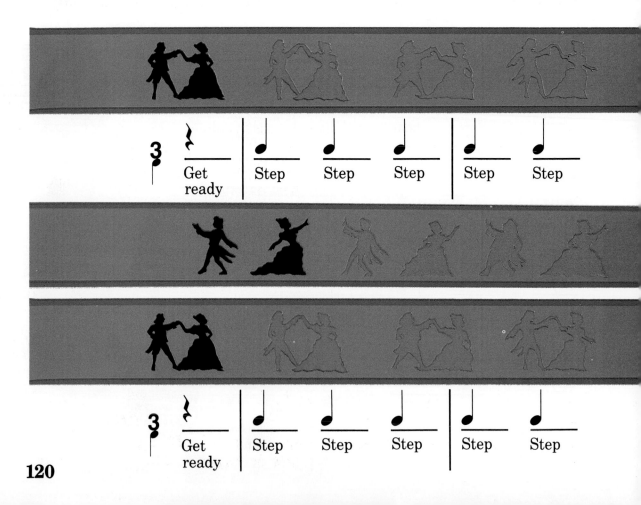

About the Music

Minuet in G was written by Ludwig van Beethoven (LOOD vihg van BAY toh vehn). In his day the minuet was a popular dance at court. The people liked it because it was easy to do.

Listen to the graceful sounds of Beethoven's music. Imagine the people dancing in their beautiful costumes. Try to keep that feeling when you dance to the music.

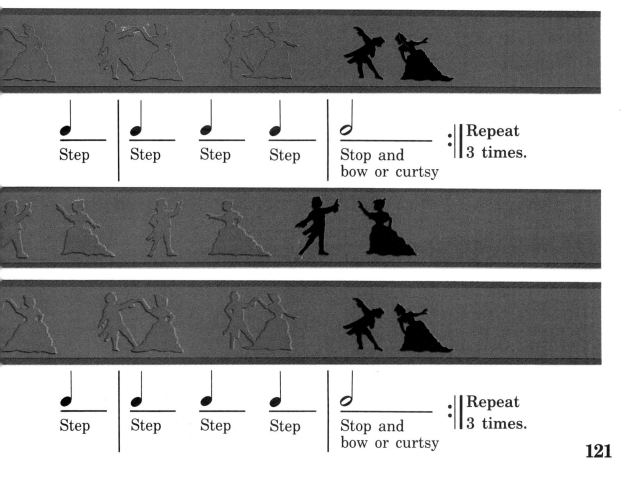

Step | Step | Step | Step | Stop and bow or curtsy | Repeat 3 times.

Step | Step | Step | Step | Stop and bow or curtsy | Repeat 3 times.

What Do You Hear 3   Fast—Slow

You will hear five pieces of music.
Listen to each piece and decide how the
music moves.

Is it all fast?

Is it all slow?

Does it change from fast to slow or from
slow to fast?

Choose your answer when the music stops.

1.   Fast   Slow   Changes

2.   Fast   Slow   Changes

3.   Fast   Slow   Changes

4.   Fast   Slow   Changes

5.   Fast   Slow   Changes

What Do You Hear 4

Instruments

Look at the pictures of the instruments. They are the clarinet, trumpet, guitar, double bass, harp, flute, and drum. You will hear three of these instruments. As the number is called, decide which instrument you hear, circle it, and put the number next to it.

clarinet ____

trumpet ____

guitar ____

double bass ____

harp ____

flute ____

drum ____

What Do You Hear 5

Step, Leap, Repeat

This exercise is in two parts. In each part you will hear three examples. On your answer sheet, circle the word <u>step</u> if the notes move by step. Circle the word <u>repeat</u> if the notes repeat. You will hear each example twice.

1.　　Step　　　　　Repeat

2.　　Step　　　　　Repeat

3.　　Step　　　　　Repeat

In the second part, circle the word <u>step</u> if the notes move by step. Circle the word <u>leap</u> if the notes move by leap.

1.　　Step　　　　　Leap

2.　　Step　　　　　Leap

3.　　Step　　　　　Leap

What Do You Hear 6

Step, Leap, Repeat

You will hear five pieces of music.
Listen to each piece and decide how the
notes move.
Do they mostly step?
Do they mostly leap?
Do they mostly repeat?

Choose your answer when the music stops.

— — — — — — — — — — — — — — —

1. Step   Leap   Repeat

2. Step   Leap   Repeat

3. Step   Leap   Repeat

4. Step   Leap   Repeat

5. Step   Leap   Repeat

Rhythm

Sometimes you can recognise a song just by its rhythm, its combination of long and short sounds. As you listen to the examples you will see the rhythm patterns written in quavers and crotchets. You will also see the titles of two songs you know. Listen as the rhythm is played and decide which song it is, then circle your answer. You will hear each pattern twice.

1.

Polly Wolly Doodle   Sandy Land

2.

Oats and Beans   In the Barnyard

3.

Rock Around My Saro Jane   Oranges and Lemons

4.

One, Two, Three, Alary   Waddaly Atcha

What Do You Hear 8

Rhythm

Each example below shows two rhythm patterns. You will hear one of them played twice. Decide which pattern you have heard and circle the answer.

1.

2.

3.

4.

5.

What Do You Hear ? 9

Rhythm Patterns

You will hear five pieces of music.
Sometimes the music has mostly even
rhythm patterns.
Other times the music has mostly uneven
rhythm patterns.

Listen to each piece and decide what
you hear.

Choose your answer when the music stops.

1.   Even   Uneven

2.   Even   Uneven

3.   Even   Uneven

4.   Even   Uneven

5.   Even   Uneven

You will hear five pieces of music.
Sometimes the music ends with a
complete phrase:

Other times the music ends partway
through a phrase:

Listen to each piece and decide what
you hear.

Choose your answer when the music stops.

1.

2.

3.

4.

5.

Form

In each example below you will hear two phrases. As you listen, decide if the phrases are the same or different, and circle your answer.

1. Same   Different

2. Same   Different

3. Same   Different

4. Same   Different

5. Same   Different

You will hear five pieces of music.
Some of the music has two sections—Ⓐ🅱.
The other piece of music has three sections—
Ⓐ🅱Ⓐ.
Listen to each piece and decide what
you hear.
Choose your answer when the music stops.

1.

2.

3.

4.

5.   A B A

SHARING MUSIC

A Party Game

Listen to this song.
Can you hear which section repeats?

Shoo, Fly

American Game Song

Shoo, fly, don't both - er me, Shoo, fly, don't both - er me,

Shoo, fly, don't both - er me, For I be-long to some-bod - y.

I feel, I feel, I feel, I feel like a morn - ing star,

I feel, I feel, I feel, I feel, I feel like a morn - ing star. So,

Shoo, fly, don't both - er me, Shoo, fly, don't both - er me,

Shoo, fly, don't both - er me, For I be-long to some-bod - y.

An Action Song

You can perform actions with this song.
The pictures will help you.

my

hat

three

corners

My Hat

Folk Song from Germany

My hat it has three cor - ners; ____

Three cor - ners has my hat; ____

And had it not three cor - ners, ____

It would not be my hat. ____

Clap and Chant

Listen for your name in this chant.
Can you say your part at the right time?

Cookie Jar

Playground Chant

All

Zoom, zoom, zoom, my heart goes ka - boom.

Now who stole the cook - ie from the cook - ie jar?

One Child

(Name) stole the cook - ie from the cook - ie jar.

Child Named   *All*

Who, me? Yes, you!

Child Named   *All*

Could - n't be! Then who?

From the Old West

Long ago, cowhands drove cattle along a
trail from Texas to Kansas, U.S.A.
The trail was long, and the work was hard.

Think how the cowhands felt as they
'pressed along' to Kansas.

Show that feeling as you sing the song.

The Big Corral

American Cowboy Song

The hus - ky brute from the cat - tle chute,

Press a - long to the big cor - ral!

He should be brand - ed on the snoot,

Press a - long to the big cor - ral!

B REFRAIN

Press a - long, cow - boy,

Press a - long with a cow - boy yell, Ya - hoo!

Press a - long, cow - boy,

Press a - long to the big cor - ral!

Play this chime bar part during section A.

Bells

R.

L.

F C D C   G C D C

F C D C

Play the woodblock during section B.
Play this steady-beat pattern or make up your
own pattern.

Play 4 times.

Hush! Child Sleeping

How will you sing this song, loud or soft?
Why?

Lullaby, My Jamie

Folk Song from Latvia   Words by Rose Stanfield

D MIN   D MIN

1. Lul - la - by, my   Ja - mie,

D MIN   D MIN

Soft - ly   sleep, my   child,

D MIN   D MIN

Sis - ter gent - ly   rocks   you,

A₇   D MIN

Light her hands and   mild.

Reproduced by permission of Novello and Company Limited

2. Snow-white lambs for Jamie,
    All kinds for your own,
    Curly, bobtailed, longtailed,
    When a man you're grown.

142

Play the autoharp with a friend
as others sing.
The chord names in the music
will help you.

Listen to this music.
Is the mood calm and gentle?

 'Invocation of the Powerful Spirits'
from Panambé . . . . Ginastera

Where Is the Flower?

The Flower (*El florón*)

Singing Game from Puerto Rico   English Words by Verne Muñoz

Pass the flow - er round and a - round.

Will it be found? Will it be found?

Pass the flow - er round and a - round.

Will it be found? Will it be found? ___

Where is it? Where is it? Where can the flow - er be? ___

Where is it? Where is it? Where can the flow - er be? ___

El florón pasó por aquí,
Yo no lo vi, Yo no lo vi. } *2 times*

¿Que pase, que pase,
Que pase el florón? } *2 times*

144

A Folk Dance

Ach ja!

Folk Song from Germany

A

When my fa - ther and my moth - er make a vis - it to the fair,

Ach ja! Ach ja!

Though they have - n't an - y mon - ey, they're as rich as an - y there,

Ach ja! Ach ja!

B REFRAIN

Tra la la, tra la la, tra la la la la la la,

Tra la la, tra la la, tra la la la la la la.

Ach ja! Ach ja!

145

Saying Goodbye

You can play the autoharp
with this song.

Which chords will you play?

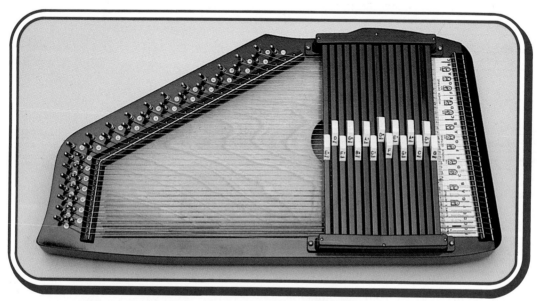

Go Well and Safely

Zulu Parting Song   English Words by Olcutt Sanders

Go   well ___ and   safe - ly,

Go   well ___ and   safe - ly,

Go   well___ and   safe - ly,

The   Lord   be   ev - er   with   you. ___

Ha-mba-ni ka-hle,
Ha-mba-ni ka-hle,
Ha-mba-ni ka-hle,
I nko-ni ma-yi-be na-ni.

A Toe-Tapping Song

Sing and dance to 'Jubilee!'

Jubilee!

Singing Game from Kentucky

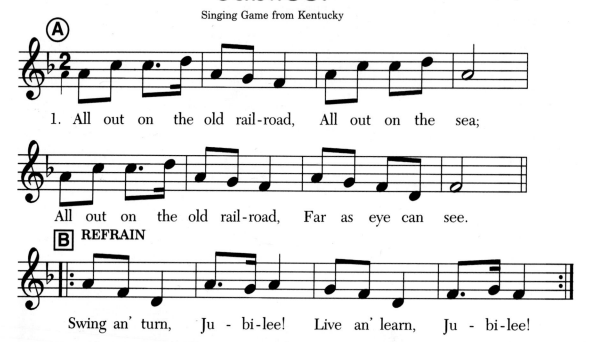

1. All out on the old rail-road, All out on the sea;

All out on the old rail-road, Far as eye can see.

B REFRAIN

Swing an' turn, Ju - bi-lee! Live an' learn, Ju - bi-lee!

2. Hardest work I've ever done,
   Workin' on the farm;
   Easiest work I've ever done,
   Swingin' my true love's arm! *Refrain*

3. If I had me a needle and thread,
   Fine as I could sew,
   Sew my true love to my side,
   And down this creek I'd go. *Refrain*

4. If I had no horse to ride,
   I'd be found a-crawlin',
   Up and down this rocky road,
   Looking for my darlin'. *Refrain*

5. All out on the old railroad,
   All out on the sea;
   All out on the old railroad,
   Far as eye can see. *Refrain*

148

Ronde and Saltarello

This music is dance music.

Listen to the recording. Do you think the dance was like the ones we do today?

6 Ronde........................Susato

Try to follow the score as you listen again.

Ⓐ

1.

2.

3.

4.
: Repeat
section A.

Ⓑ

1.

2.
: Repeat
section B.

Now listen to the same music played a different way.

6 Saltarello....................Susato

About the Music

Ronde and Saltarello are dance pieces. They were written in the 1500s by Tielman Susato (TEEL mahn soo ZAH toh). Susato did not say which instruments should play the dances. He wanted them played on any instruments that the people had. You have heard the dances played on brass instruments. How do you think they would sound on flutes? Or on violins? Or on guitar? They would sound fine on almost any instrument.

Ronde and Saltarello are really two names for the same music. Both pieces have the same melody, but they use it in different ways. Listen to the pieces, one after the other. Notice the special feeling that each piece has.

Dance a Song

Listen for two different sections in this song. Which is repeated—A or B?

Run, Children, Run

Black American Folk Song   Words Adapted

Run, chil-dren, run,   it's   time to hur - ry home now;

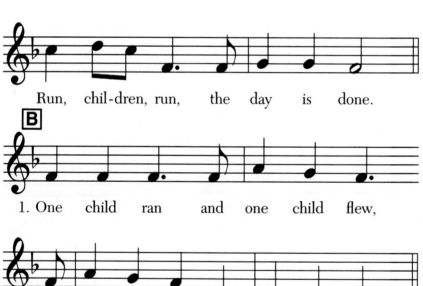

Run, chil-dren, run,   the   day   is   done.

1. One   child   ran   and   one   child   flew,

And   one   child   lost   a   Sun - day   shoe.

Run, chil-dren, run,   it's   time to hur - ry home now;

Run, chil-dren, run,   the   day   is   done.

From AMERICAN FOLK SONGS FOR CHILDREN (Ruth Crawford Seeger). Copyright 1925 by Harvard University Press, © 1953 by Mary McDaniel Parker. Reprinted by permission of Harvard University Press.

2. Let me tell you what I'll do:
   I'm going to find my
      Sunday shoe.

3. Let me tell you where I'll be:
   I'm going to look
      behind that tree.

Listen for the sections in this music.

'Run, Run' from Memories of
Childhood . . . . Pinto

A Song to Sign

Sign language helps us speak to people who cannot hear.
Look at the pictures on page 155.
They show the signs for the words in this song.

My Father's House

Traditional American Song

1.–3. Won't you come with me   to   my   fa-ther's house,

To   my   fa-ther's house,   to   my   fa-ther's house?

Oh,   won't you come with   me   to   my   fa-ther's house,

1. There   is   peace,   peace,   peace.

2. . . . There is joy, joy, joy.

3. . . . There is love, love, love.

Try to 'sign' the song as you sing.

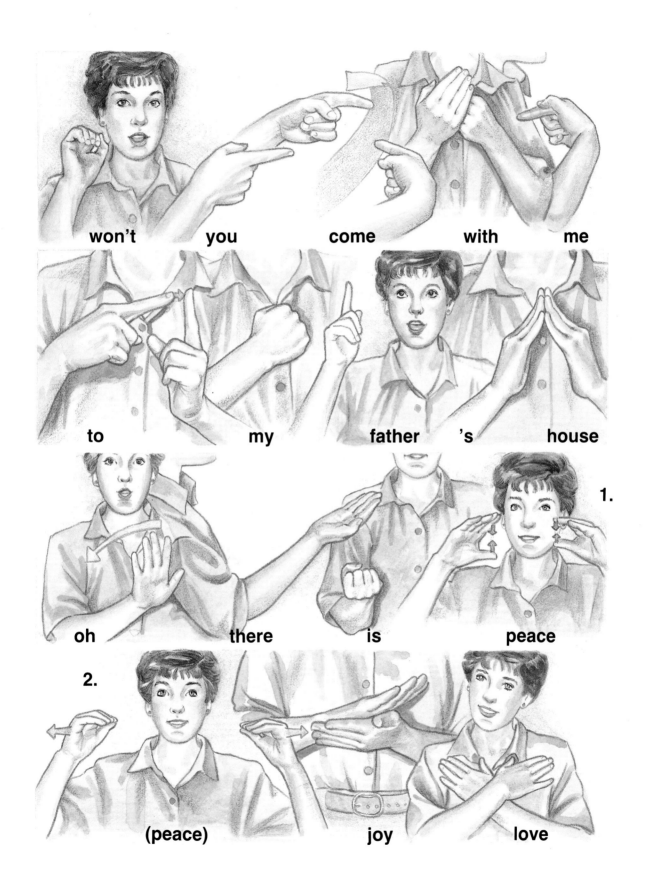

won't you come with me

to my father's house

oh there is peace

1.

2. (peace) joy love

155

A Quiet Time

American Indian children take part in
the songs and dances of their nation.
At an early age they learn how to
beat a drum.
They also learn to shake rattles.

Sunset

North American Indian Song

Now the   moon ___   is   in   the   sky,

To   the   sun ___   we   say good-bye;

Fa-ther Sun   sleeps   in   the   West.

In   the   sky ___   we   see   the   moon;

Shad-ows   creep, ___ the night comes soon;

Fa - ther Sun sleeps in the West,

And his peo - ple go to ___ rest.

Play the steady beat on a tom-tom.

Repeat over and over.

Add these parts when you can.

Repeat over and over.

Repeat over and over.

An Add-On Song

You can create sound effects for this song.
Choose sounds that you like.

Goat Song

Folk Song from Italy English Words by Leo Israel
Collected and Adapted by Rudolph Goehr

1. Oh, the goat came skip-ping, From the pas-ture trip-ping,

And he ate my shoe; Oh, ___ he nib-bled at my shoe!

Then he gob-bled up my shoe!

What to do with just one shoe! ___

2. Then the wolf came howling,
When the goat came skipping,
From the pasture tripping,
And he ate my shoe;
Oh, he nibbled at my shoe!
Then he gobbled up my shoe!
What to do with just one shoe!

3. Then the dog came barking,
    When the wolf came howling,
    When the goat came skipping . . .

4. Then the stick came beating,
    When the dog came barking,
    When the wolf came howling,
    When the goat came skipping . . .

5. Then a fire was burning,
    When the stick came beating,
    When the dog came barking,
    When the wolf came howling,
    When the goat came skipping . . .

6. With the water pouring,
    When a fire was burning,
    When the stick came beating,
    When the dog was barking,
    When the wolf came howling,
    When the goat came skipping . . .

7. And I lay there sleeping,
    With the water pouring,
    When a fire was burning,
    When the stick came beating,
    When the dog came barking,
    When the wolf came howling,
    When the goat came skipping . . .

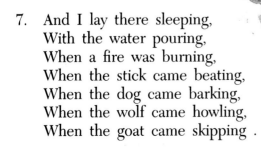

Finding a Pattern

Look for this short-short-long pattern in the song:

♩ ♩ 𝅗𝅥

How many times do you see it?

Old John Braddelum

Folk Melody from England Words Adapted

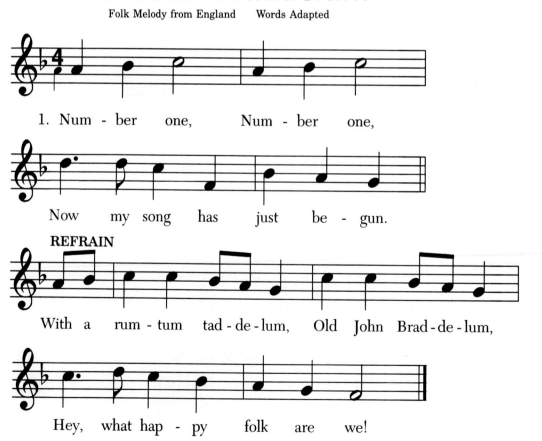

1. Num - ber   one,   Num - ber   one,

Now   my   song   has   just   be - gun.

REFRAIN

With   a   rum - tum   tad - de - lum,   Old   John   Brad - de - lum,

Hey,   what   hap - py   folk   are   we!

2. Number two, Number two,
   You're with me and I'm with you.
   Refrain

3. Number three, Number three,
   This is easy as can be.
   Refrain

4. Number four, Number four,
   Just keep singing—we want more!
   Refrain

5. Number five, Number five,
   It's so great to be alive!
   Refrain

Play the ♩ ♩ ♩ pattern on a percussion instrument.

LISTENING SKILLS 6 Staines Morris Dance (excerpt) . . . . **Anonymous**

Listen for the tambourine in this music. Which set of lines below shows the pattern it plays?

1. — — ——   **2.** —— — —

Sing and Speak

Have you ever made a peanut-butter-and-jelly sandwich this way?

Peanut Butter

Camp Song

Pea - nut, _ pea-nut but - ter, _ jel - ly!

VERSE

1. First you dig the pea - nuts, and you dig 'em, you dig 'em.

You dig 'em, dig 'em, dig 'em, then you crush 'em, you crush 'em.

You crush 'em, crush 'em, crush 'em, then you spread 'em, you spread 'em.

You spread 'em, spread 'em, spread 'em. *Refrain*

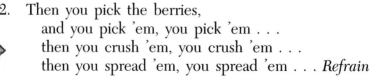

2. Then you pick the berries,
   and you pick 'em, you pick 'em . . .
   then you crush 'em, you crush 'em . . .
   then you spread 'em, you spread 'em . . . *Refrain*

3. Then you bite the sandwich,
   and you bite it, you bite it . . .
   and you munch it, you munch it, . . .
   then you swallow, you swallow . . . *Refrain*

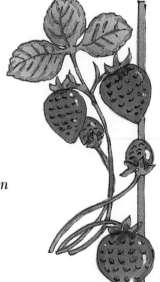

Rhythm Patterns to Play

How Good and Joyous

Hebrew Folk Song

How good and joy - ous it is _____

For broth - ers to dwell to - geth - er.

Good and joy - ous

For broth - ers to dwell to - geth - er.

Hi-neh mah tov u-ma na-im,
She-vet a-chim gam ya-chad. } 2 times
Hi-neh mah tov,
She-vet a-chim gam ya-chad. } 2 times

You can play these rhythm patterns to accompany the song.

1. Repeat over and over.

2. Repeat over and over.

3. Repeat over and over.

A Musical Scene

Children in China sing about things they
see outside.
Which words in the song tell you this?

What sounds does the song tell about?
Listen for them on the recording.

Temple Bell

Melody from China   Words from a Chinese Poem   Adapted by Burton Kurth

1. Moun-tains hid in a mist-y cloud;

Bam-boos lin-ing the dust-y road.

Chim-ing call of tem-ple bell;

Night is fall-ing on field and dell.

2. Homeward come the weary feet
Trudging down the village street,
Welcomed by the sound of flute.
Soon, oh, soon will all sounds be mute.

Now listen to this music from China.
It suggests the rising and the setting of
the moon.

LISTENING SKILLS 6 **Chinese: High Moon**

165

The Snow Is Dancing

Have you ever sat by a window and
watched the snow fall?
Did you notice changes as it fell?

Sometimes the snow swirls.

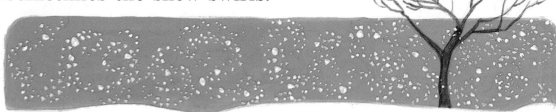

Sometimes it drops like a heavy curtain.

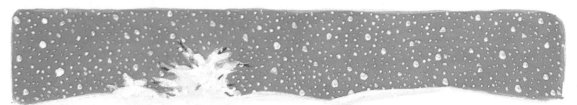

Sometimes the flakes dance.

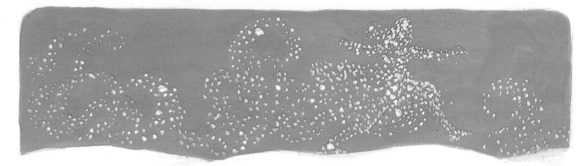

Listen to this music.
Try to picture the dancing snow.

 'The Snow Is Dancing' from Children's
Corner Suite . . . . Debussy

These lines show the shape of three melodies.
Can you hear the melodies in the music?

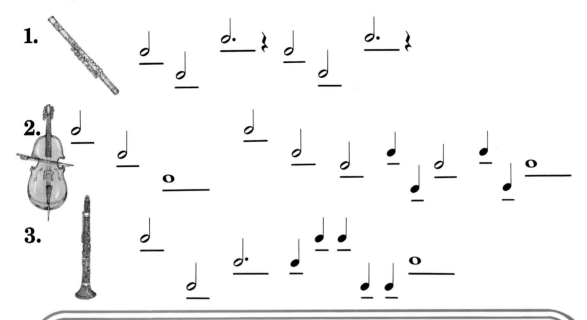

About the Music

Can you imagine a piece of music being a present? That's what 'The Snow Is Dancing' was. This music is part of a larger work called Children's Corner Suite. Claude Debussy (klohd deh byew see) wrote Children's Corner Suite as a present for his daughter. There are five other pieces in Children's Corner Suite. One of them is a lullaby for an elephant. Another one is a lively dance called 'Golliwog's Cakewalk.' How happy the little girl must have been with her present!

A Story Song

Market Song

Folk Song from Italy   English Words by Leo Israel
Collected and Adapted by Rudolph Goehr

All

1. One day my moth - er went to the mar - ket

And she bought a hand - some roost - er.

Solo   *Chorus*

A roost - er?   A roost - er!

All

But when my moth - er start - ed to cook him,

He did ev' - ry - thing he use - ta.

Solo   *Chorus*

He use - ta?   He use - ta!

All

Oh, he said, 'Cock - a - doo - dle - doo,

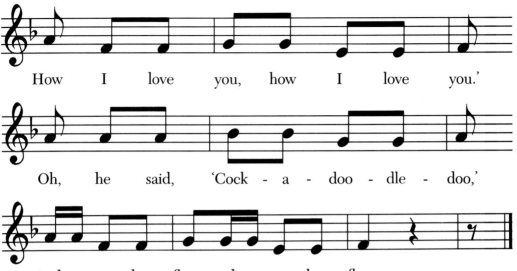

How I love you, how I love you.'

Oh, he said, 'Cock - a - doo - dle - doo,'

And a - way he flew, and a - way he flew.

2. . . . and she bought a little pig . . .
    But when my mother started to cook him,
    He got up and danced a jig . . .
    Oh, he said, 'Oink, oink, oink,
    Though I'd like to stay, though I'd like to stay.'
    Oh, he said, 'Oink, oink, oink,'
    And he ran away, and he ran away.

3. . . . and she bought a pretty lamb . . .
    But when my mother started to cook him,
    He said, 'Who do you think I am?' . . .
    Oh, he said, 'Baa, baa, baa,
    I'm silly, it's true, I'm silly, it's true.'
    Oh, he said, 'Baa, baa, baa,
    Not as silly as you, not as silly as you.'

4. . . . and she bought a lovely hen . . .
    But when my mother started to cook her,
    She began to cluck again . . .
    Oh, she said, 'Cluck, cluck, cluck, cluck, cluck.'
    But she forgot, but she forgot,
    Oh, she said, 'Cluck, cluck, cluck, cluck, cluck,'
    And fell into the pot, and fell into the pot.

Hoot and Holler!

Listen for the sound effects in this song.
Try to perform them with the recording.

She'll Be Comin' Round the Mountain

Southern Mountain Song

1. She'll be com - in' round the moun - tain when she comes, _____ *(Toot, toot!)*

She'll be com - in' round the moun - tain when she comes, _____ *(Toot, toot!)*

She'll be com - in' round the moun - tain,

She'll be com - in' round the moun - tain,

She'll be com - in' round the moun - tain when she comes. _____ *(Toot, toot!)*

2. She'll be drivin' six white horses when she comes,
   (*Whoa, back!*)

3. Oh, we'll kill the old red rooster when she comes,
   (*Chop, chop!*)

4. Oh, we'll all have chicken and dumplin's when she comes,
   (*Yum, yum!*)

5. Oh, we'll all go out to meet her when she comes,
   (*Hi, there!*)

A Surprise

Have you ever had a surprise?
Did something happen that you did
not expect?

In this song something unexpected comes
from a root.
Listen to discover what it is.

From a Lovely Root

Yiddish Folk Song   English Words by Elizabeth S. Bachman

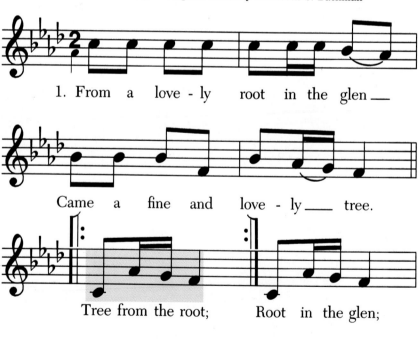

1. From a love - ly root in the glen ___

Came a fine and love - ly ___ tree.

Tree from the root;   Root in the glen;

So it is now and ev - er has been.

2. On the tree that came from the root
   Grew a fine and lovely branch.
   Branch on the tree;
   Tree from the root;
   Root in the glen;
   So it is now and ever has been.

3. On the branch that grew on the tree
   Sat a fine and lovely nest.
   Nest on the branch . . .

4. In the nest that sat on the branch
   Sang a fine and lovely bird.
   Bird in the nest . . .

5. On the bird that sang in the nest
   Grew some fine and lovely feathers.
   Feathers on the bird . . .

6. From the lovely feathers on the bird
   Came a fine and lovely pillow.
   Pillow from the feathers . . .

173

Wake Up!

Every morning starts a new day.

How does the person in this song
feel each morning?
Which words tell you so?

Every Mornin'

Words and Music by Avon Gillespie

C   G

Ev - e - ry morn - in' when I wake — up

E   C

I have a new song to sing, my chil - dren,

C   G

Ev - e - ry morn - in' when I wake — up

E   C

I have a new song to sing.

Play a chime bar part while others sing
'Every Mornin'.'

Follow the notes in colour boxes.
The letters under the notes tell which chime
bars to play.

Let's Have a Parade!

Can you hear these instruments
on the recording?
Each one plays a different melody.

Point to the picture that shows the
instrument you hear.

piccolo

tuba

trombone

trumpet

The Very Best Band

Words and Music by Joe Hampson

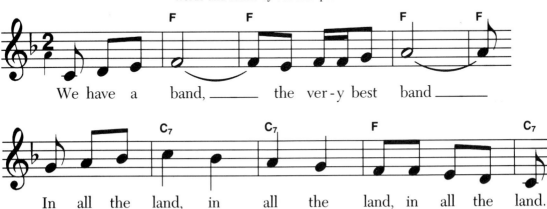

We have a band, ____ the ver-y best band ____

In all the land, in all the land, in all the land.

We have a band, ____ the ver-y best band ____

In all the land, in all the land. ____

© 1980 by Pachyderm Music, CAPAC. Reprinted by permission of Elephant Records, Inc.

The Stars and Stripes Forever (excerpt) ....Sousa

This music is often played by parade bands.
Listen for the sound of the piccolo.
Does the piccolo play the same melody as
the other instruments?

Tone Colour

Listen as each number is called. You will see the names of two instruments, but you will hear only one. Decide which instrument you hear and circle its name.

1. Autoharp   Piano

2. Violin   Woodblock

3. Trumpet   Xylophone

4. Piano   Tambourine

5. Triangle   Tambourine

What Do You Hear ? 14

Tone Colour

As you look at each number below you will see pictures of two different instruments. Listen as each number is called and decide which instrument you hear, then circle the instrument's picture.

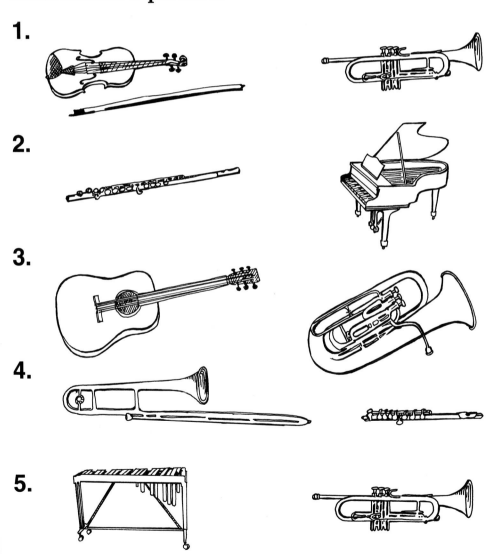

1.

2.

3.

4.

5.

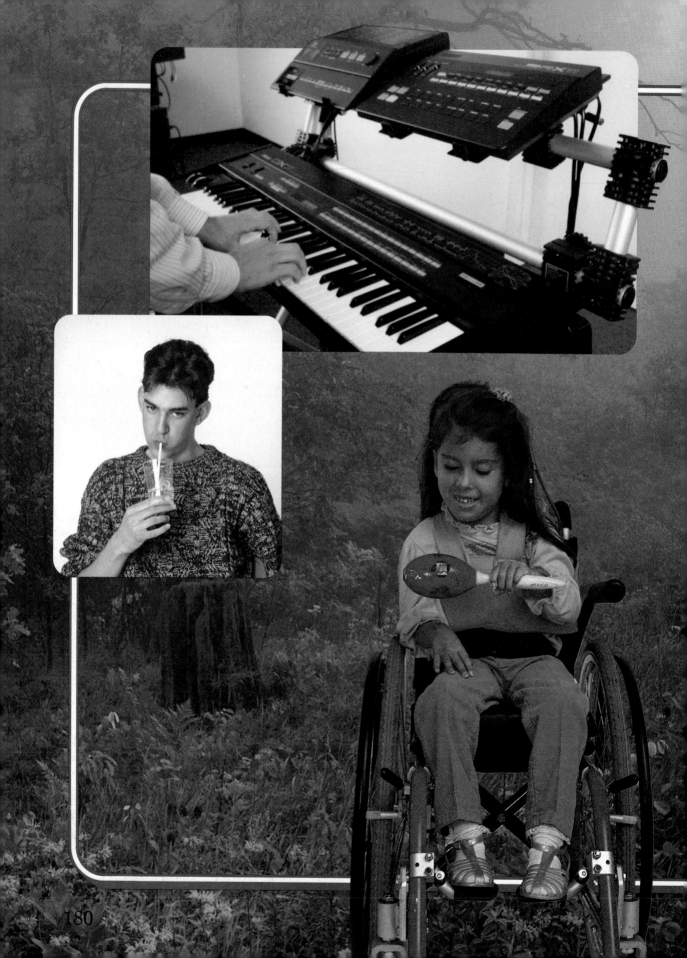

The Sounds of the Pied Piper

Long ago in Germany
the town of Hameln had a terrible problem.

RATS!

They filled the streets and houses of the town.
So the mayor offered a reward
to anyone who could get rid of the rats.
Soon a strange man
dressed in red and yellow appeared.
He carried a little melody pipe.

'My pipe can charm these rats,' he said,
and he put the pipe to his lips.
The melody was full of magic.
It swooped up and down.
Long and short notes tumbled from his pipe.
At the first notes the rats
left the shops and houses
and followed the piper through the streets
and down into the river.

The mayor was pleased
but he was also a very mean man,
so when the piper came to claim his reward
the mayor said, 'I will not pay you
for such an easy trick!'

'I have other tricks, too,' warned the piper.

What the Pied Piper Did

The piper put his pipe to his lips again.
This time the melody was so jolly,
tripping and skipping, that all the children
in the town ran from their homes
and formed a procession behind the piper
as he played.

Through the streets they danced and sang,
across the fields and forests
to the mountains.

There a great door appeared in the rocks and all the children ran inside. The door closed and children and piper were never seen again.

How do you think the Pied Piper's melodies sounded?
How did the rats' melody sound?
Was it different from the children's melody?

Whisker WHISPER
sss SQUEAL
scrimple scramble SCRUNCH
SCAT squeak
PITTER-PATTER SKITTER-SKATTER
scrabble SCROBBLE squeak

Listen to two melodies on two sorts of pipes.
One pipe is a flute.
The other is an oboe.

Syrinx (for solo flute)
........Debussy

Phaeton (for solo oboe)
........Britten

rrrrrrrrrRRRATS

185

The Story of Petrouchka

Sing this Russian song about a puppet.

Puppet Dance

Folk Song from Russia   English Words by George Odam

Wood - en legs, wood - en feet in wood - en shoes,

Step - ping all a - round when your mast - ers choose.

Wood - en eyes, wood - en smile and wood - en frown, You

dance a hap - py step be - fore you sit right down.

"Russian Puppet Dance" from *PETROUCHKA* by Igor Stravinsky. Used by permission of Boosey & Hawkes, Inc.

In a fairground in old Russia, there stood
a puppet theatre.
Three puppets danced in the theatre.
Petrouchka was a sad clown.
Columbine danced to the side of Petrouchka.
She was a pretty ballerina from Italy.
The Moor, a strong warrior from Morocco,
danced to the side of Columbine.

Listen to the orchestra playing the music
the puppets dance to. Do you recognise it?
Is it slower, faster, or the same speed
as when you sang it?

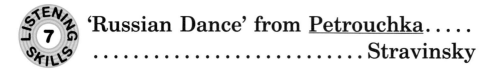

'Russian Dance' from <u>Petrouchka</u>.....
.... Stravinsky

Did Igor Stravinsky use steps, leaps, or both?

Can you make up a melody
for Columbine? Use these notes.

Will you use steps? Leaps?
Both steps and leaps?

Can you make up a melody
for the Moor? Use these notes.

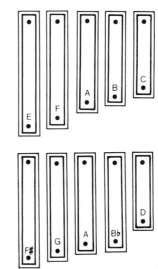

Going 'Like This' from China

After you learn this song,
your teacher can show you some actions
to do with it.
Don't get muddled!

My Ship Sailed from China

Folk Song from England

My ship sailed from Chi - na with a car - go of tea,

It was lad - en with pres - ents for you and for me;

It brought me a fan, Just im - a - gine my bliss,

When I found my - self go - ing like this,

Like this, like this, like this.

Work with some friends to 'load up'
a musical ship.
Load it up with a musical cargo
and then 'unload' it.

When the ship is loaded, set sail
by singing the song.
At the end you can unload the cargo,
box by box.

An Adventure with Alice

from <u>Through the Looking-Glass</u>, by Lewis Carroll

The messenger handed a sandwich to the King.

'I'll whisper it,' said the messenger,
putting his hands to his mouth in the shape
of a trumpet and stooping so as to get close
to the King's ear.
Alice was sorry for this, as she wanted to hear
the news, too.
However, instead of whispering,
he simply shouted at the top of his voice,

'They're at it again!'

'Do you call that a whisper?' cried the poor King,
jumping up and shaking himself.
'If you do such a thing again, I'll have you buttered!
It went through my head like an earthquake!'

'It would have to be a very tiny earthquake!'
thought Alice.
'Who are at it again?' she ventured to ask.

'Why, the Lion and the Unicorn, of course,' said the King.

'Fighting for the crown!'
'Yes to be sure,' said the King.
'And the best joke is
that it's my crown all the while!
Let's run and see them.'

And they trotted off, Alice repeating to herself,
as she ran, the words of the old song:

'The Lion and the Unicorn
were fighting for the crown:
The Lion beat the Unicorn
all round the town.
Some gave them white bread,
some gave them brown.
Some gave them plum-cake
and drummed them out of town.'

Making an Alice Song

On page 191, Alice repeated a song to herself.
Can you invent a melody for the song?
Try using these notes.

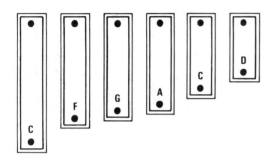

Add other notes if you need them.

Drums for Alice

The Lion said 'Do you like
plum-cake, Monster?'
But before Alice could answer
him, the drums began.

Where the noise came from
she couldn't make out:
the air seemed full of it,
and it rang through and
through her till she felt
quite deafened.

Perhaps you could act out the scene you read
on pages 190, 191, and 193.
How will the scene finish?
Look at the illustration to get an idea.
You will need many instruments,
but they are all much alike.
What kinds of instruments are they?

The Lobster Quadrille

A <u>quadrille</u> is a very complicated dance.
What if it were danced by fishes, snails, and lobsters?
It would be even more complicated!
Can you invent a good melody to finish the song?

The Lobster Quadrille

Words by Lewis Carroll   Music Traditional

VERSE *Solo*

'Will you walk a lit-tle fast-er?' said a whit-ing to a snail,

'There's a por-poise close be-hind us and he's tread-ing on my tail.

See how eag-er-ly the lob-sters and the tur-tles all ad-vance!

They are wait-ing on the shin-gle Will you come and join the dance?'

REFRAIN
Chorus

Will you, won't you, will you, won't you, Will you join the dance?

Will you, won't you, will you, won't you, Won't you join the dance?

2.   'You can really have no notion how delightful it will
         be
     When they take us up and throw us, with the lobsters, out to
         sea!'
     But the snail replied, 'Too far, too far!' and gave a look
         askance —
     Said he thanked the whiting kindly, but he would not join
         the dance.
         Would not, could not, would not, could not, would not
             join the dance.
         Would not, could not, would not, could not, could not
             join the dance.

3.   'What matters it how far we go?' his scaly friend replied.
     'There is another shore, you know, upon the other side.
     The further off from England the nearer is to France —
     Then turn not pale, beloved snail, but come and join the
         dance.
         Will you, won't you, will you, won't you, will you join
             the dance?
         Will you, won't you, will you, won't you, won't you join
             the dance?'

An African Fable

The Animals Make a Drum

Children in Africa know a story
about animals in the forest.

A long time ago, Lion, who lived in the wild jungle forest,
called together his friends Leopard, Giraffe,
Cheetah, and Elephant.
'Welcome, welcome,' said Lion.
'Can you help me make a drum?'
The animals thought and thought.
Leopard said, 'I will dig out the inside of an old log.'
And he did.
Lion beat the hollow log with a stick.
And the animals listened.
They heard thud, THUD!

196

Lion said, 'How can we make this drum sing?'
The animals thought and thought.
Cheetah said, 'Do we have something to stretch
over the top of the log to make it sing?'

The animals thought and thought.

Giraffe stood tall and said, 'Elephant has big ears.
They would cover the hollow log.'

Elephant said, 'I will give one of my ears,
but you must give one, too.'

Playing Drums

A-tin-go-tin

Folk Song from Nigeria   As Sung by Soloman Ilori   Words Adapted

Chorus

A - tin - go - tin,   A - tin - go - tin,   A - tin - go - tin,   A - tin - go - tin.

Leader   *Chorus*   *Leader*

Ti - ri - rin - go - tin,   A - tin - go - tin.   All the beasts, here and there.

Chorus   *Leader*   *Chorus*   *Leader*

A - tin - go - tin, Must give one ear,   A - tin - go - tin, To make a   drum,

Chorus   *Leader*   *Chorus*   *Leader*

A - tin - go - tin, So we can dance. A - tin - go - tin. Ti - ri - rin - go - tin,

Chorus

A - tin - go - tin,   A - tin - go - tin,   A - tin - go - tin,   A - tin - go - tin.

Find three drum sounds—low, middle, and high.
Can you imitate the melody pattern
of the word <u>A-tin-go-tin?</u>

Play your drums to accompany the song.
Remember, the pattern is low-middle-high-middle.
Can you make a drum?

The Animals Finish the Drum

No one knew how to play the drum.
Lion said, 'Monkey is a clever fellow.
I will ask him to show us how to play the drum.'

Lion said, 'Monkey, show us how to play it.'
Monkey's long fingers made some music on the drum.

All the animals in turn played monkey's drum music.
They thanked Monkey with this song.

Kawakayima

Traditional

VERSE

1. Li - on ver - y brave and Buff'-lo ver - y strong,

Chee - tah ver - y fast and Py - thon ver - y long,

REFRAIN

Ka - wa - ka - yi - ma, ver - y weak and small,

Such a clev - er Mon - key, the smart-est of them all.

2. Jackal very wicked, Hippo very tough,
   Elephant is huge and Rhino very rough. *Refrain*

Collect as many drums as you can.
Make sure they are different sizes.
Can you make 'sound pictures' of the
animals in the story?

Think how Elephant walks
and moves.
Will you choose low drum sounds
or high drum sounds?
Make some sound patterns
on your drums
to imitate Elephant.

Think how Leopard runs
and hunts. First he waits.
He wriggles.
Then he runs fast and pounces.
What drum sounds will you use?
Make some sound patterns
to imitate Leopard.

Think how Monkey jumps
and swings through the trees.
Often he disappears,
only to jump out again.
He is full of surprises.
How will Monkey's
drum music sound?

Work out some ideas for your drum music.
Practise your ideas until you feel
you are ready to play for others.
Ask your friends to listen and guess
which animal your drums are describing.
Listen to the sound of real drums from Africa.

Tanzanian Drums

An Old Motor Car

Listen for the sound of an old motor car.

Chitty Chitty Bang Bang

Words and Music by Richard M. Sherman and Robert B. Sherman

Oh! You pre - ty chit - ty bang, bang,

Chit - ty Chit - ty Bang Bang, we love you.

And our pret - ty chit - ty bang, bang,

Chit - ty Chit - ty Bang Bang loves us too!

Near, far, in our mo - tor car,

Oh, what a hap - py time we'll spend.

Bang, bang, Chit - ty Chit - ty Bang Bang!

to Coda

Our fine four - fen - dered friend.

You're uncategorical;
A fuel burning oracle,
A fantasmagorical machine.
You're more than spectacular,
To use the vernacular,
You're wizard! You're smashing! You're keen! *D.C. al Coda*

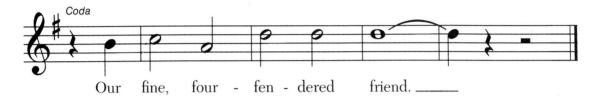

Our fine,   four - fen - dered   friend. _____

Can you think of some chitty-chitty sounds
to make?
Look at the picture.
Which parts of the car are making sounds?
How can you imitate the sounds in music?

Sounds Near and Far

Listen to this piece.
It is about a wagon passing by.
The wagon is drawn by a cart horse.
How does the composer help you to imagine
the wagon passing?
You hear it coming near, passing by,
then going away.

LISTENING SKILLS 8

'The Wagon Passes' from <u>Nursery
Suite</u> . . . . Elgar

Can you invent some sound pictures for these?
Will each sound picture seem to start
from far away?
Will it seem to get nearer?
Will it seem to pass by
and go away?

Toad's First Car

from <u>The Wind in the Willows</u>, by Kenneth Grahame

They were strolling along the high road easily,
the Mole by the horse's head, talking to him,
since the horse had complained
that he was being frightfully left out of it,
and nobody considered him in the least;
the Toad and the Water Rat walking behind
the cart talking together—at least Toad was talking,
and Rat was saying at intervals,
'Yes, precisely; and what did <u>you</u> say to <u>him</u>?'—
and thinking all the time of something very different,
when far behind them they heard a faint warning hum,
like the drone of a distant bee.
Glancing back, they saw a small cloud of dust,
with a dark centre of energy,
advancing on them at incredible speed,
while from out of the dust a faint 'Poop-poop!'
wailed like an uneasy animal in pain.
Hardly regarding it, they turned to resume their conversation,
when in an instant (as it seemed)
the peaceful scene was changed,
and with a blast of wind
and a whirl of sound that made them jump
for the nearest ditch,
it was on them!

The 'poop-poop' rang with a brazen shout
in their ears,
they had a moment's glimpse of an interior
of glittering plate-glass and rich morocco,
and the magnificent motor-car, immense, breath-snatching,
passionate, with its pilot tense and hugging his wheel,
possessed all earth and air for the fraction of a second,
flung an enveloping cloud of dust
that blinded and enwrapped them utterly,
and then dwindled to a speck in the far distance,
changed back into a droning bee once more.

Can you make up a song about Toad
and the car?
Here are some words you can use
if you like.

> Mister Toad saw a car,
> Saw it coming from afar,
> Shiny bright, spanking new,
> Toad said, 'I shall have one, too!
> One with lots of chrome appeals,
> Gleaming paint and shining wheels!
> Leather cover on the steering,
> Bulbous horn to test one's hearing;
> Lovely as a car can be
> To carry Rat and Mole and me.'

Use these notes:

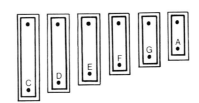

You can use this music as
a first line, if you wish.

Mis - ter Toad saw a car, Saw it com - ing from a - far.

A Picture in Sound

Can you make a sound picture
of Toad's first meeting with a motor car?
There are many sounds
in the story—horse and cart,
a motor car far away and coming nearer,
a faint warning hum, a 'poop-poop!'

You may hear other sounds in the story.
How will you organise your sounds?
You could begin with the horse and cart.
You could begin with the motor car
coming and going.
Perhaps you can think of another way to begin.

Can you make a chart to show
how your sound picture goes?
What sorts of symbols will you need?
You will need a symbol for each sound.
Here are a few symbols.
What sounds do they make you think of?

Not all these symbols may be useful to you.
Can you think of other symbols
to represent your sounds?

Mole Discovers a River

He thought his happiness was complete when,
as he meandered aimlessly along,
suddenly he stood by the edge of a full-fed river.
Never in his life had he seen a river before—
this sleek, sinuous, full-bodied animal,
chasing and chuckling, gripping things with a gurgle
and leaving them with a laugh,
to fling itself on fresh playmates
that shook themselves free,
and were caught and held again.
All was a-shake and a-shiver—glints and gleams
and sparkles, rustle and swirl, chatter and bubble.
The Mole was bewitched, entranced, fascinated.
By the side of the river he trotted
as one trots, when very small, by the side
of a man who holds one spellbound
by exciting stories; and when tired at last,
he sat on the bank, while the river
still chattered on to him, a babbling procession

of the best stories in the world,
sent from the heart of the earth
to be told at last
to the insatiable sea.

Here is a song Mole might have sung
if he had only known it.

The River

Music by Bedrich Smetana   Words by George Odam

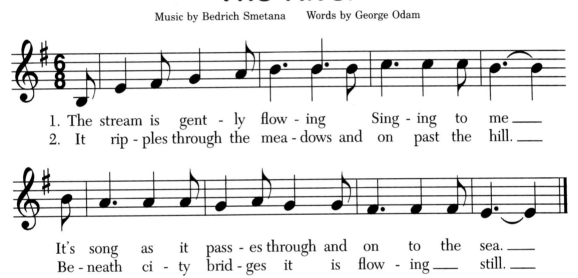

1. The stream is gent - ly flow - ing   Sing - ing to me ____
2. It rip - ples through the mea - dows and on past the hill. ____

It's song as it pass - es through and on to the sea. ____
Be - neath ci - ty brid - ges it is flow - ing ___ still. ____

Mole was fascinated by the river.
Some composers have been fascinated by rivers.
Listen to some music written to describe
a river in Bohemia.

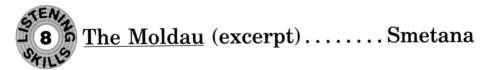 The Moldau (excerpt) . . . . Smetana

Can you think of some sounds
to go along with The Moldau?
A glissando on the xylophone
might show the river's flow.

211

Working with Recorded Sound

Mole cannot see very well.
Can you make a sound picture to help him?
That way, he can recognise the river
with his ears.
You can use a small portable cassette tape
recorder to record the sound of water.
Pour water into different containers—a bowl,
a sink, a bottle.
You can hear how the sound changes
in different containers. Record the sounds.
Remember how Mole
heard the rivers—
'chasing and chuckling,'
'a-shake and a-shiver.'

Record enough water sounds to last
about thirty seconds.
Listen to the recording
all the way through several times.
As you listen, think what sorts of instruments
you can add for more interest.
You might consider a cymbal with beaters,
a triangle, wind chimes, or other interesting sounds.

Work out some river sounds with these instruments.
As the tape plays, add your sounds to the picture.
Can you make a chart of your river piece?

Listen to the way one composer describes
a water-mill in music.
You can hear it turning by the still mill-pond.

8 By the Water-Mill . . . . Bynge

213

Momotaro

A Story from Japan

Long, long ago on one of the small islands
of Japan, there lived an old woodcutter
and his wife.

They were very sad because they had no children.
One day they started to work as usual.
The old man went off to the hills
to chop wood
and the old woman went down to the river
with a basket of clothes to wash.
As she worked at her washing,
she saw something floating down the river
as it splashed and gurgled on its way.

It was a large peach.
It floated nearer and nearer
until she reached it and picked it up.
She put the peach on top
of the clean washing and carried it home.

The old man was very fond of peaches and,
when he returned and saw the fine peach,
he could hardly wait
to cut it open and eat it.
But while they were looking at it,
suddenly a voice came from inside the peach:

'Wait a moment, old man!'

Suddenly the peach split in two
and there inside was a live baby boy.
The man and his wife were overjoyed
to have a son at last
and they named him Momotaro.
Momotaro is the Japanese word for
'boy from a peach.'

Momotaro grew tall and strong
and the old man and woman thought he was
the most wonderful boy in the world.

Music for a Cinema

If Momotaro were a film, it would probably
have music. Can you make some music
or sound pictures to go with 'Momotaro'?
Read the story again and try to imagine sounds
that will fit. Perhaps ideas from other places
in this book will help you.

Japan has many kinds of musical instruments.
The <u>koto</u> is one of them.
Do you remember the koto on page 73?
Look at this picture of a woman
playing a koto.
Then listen to a Japanese folk song
played on a koto.

 8 <u>Variations on 'Sakura'</u>..... Traditional

Momotaro's Journey

When Momotaro was fifteen years old,
he told his father and mother
that he must leave home for a while.
'I must go to the land where the ogres live,'
he said,
'for the ogres are bad and do great harm
in Japan. They steal cattle
and all the people's treasures.
Now that I am tall and strong,
I shall fight the ogres and drive them away!'

The old woman said, 'Go if you must,
but first take some of my fine
millet flour dumplings for your journey.'

The old man hung a bozu doll on the branches
of a willow tree to bring good weather
for Momotaro's journey.

Teru, Teru Bozu

Folk Song from Japan English Words by George Odam

Te - ru, te - ru bo - zu, Te - ru bo - zu,

Bring us good weath - er for trav - el - ling to - day;

Hang the bo - zu high so the rain will keep a - way,

Bring us — all good weath - er for trav - el - ling to - day.

Te - ru, te - ru bo - zu, Te - ru bo - zu,

Bring us good weath - er for trav - el - ling to - day.

So Momotaro set off on his journey.

Momotaro on His Way

On the way, Momotaro met the cleverest monkey
in the world.
'Where are you going?' asked the monkey.
'I am going to the ogres' island
to stop their evil tricks,' said Momotaro.
'If you will give me one of your dumplings,
I will go with you,' said the monkey.
So Momotaro gave him the first dumpling
and the monkey ran and swung along with him.

Can you make some running and
swinging music for the monkey?
Try to include scampering
and jumping sounds.

Soon they met the finest pheasant in the land.
'Where are you going?' asked the pheasant.
'I am going to the ogres' island
to stop their evil tricks,' said Momotaro.
'If you will give me a dumpling,
I will go with you,' said the pheasant,
and soon the pheasant was flying along
as the monkey swung and jumped
and Momotaro strode along.

Can you make some fluttering and squawking
sounds for the pheasant? These will be good
to go with Momotaro on his journey.

A while after this, Momotaro met
the fiercest dog in Japan.
'Where are you going?' asked the dog.
'I am going to the ogres' island
to stop their evil tricks,' said Momotaro.
'If you will give me the third dumpling,
I will come, too,' said the dog.
And soon all three friends
were journeying along.

Can you make some fierce dog music?
It might have barking
and growling sounds.

Momotaro and the cleverest monkey
and the finest pheasant
and the fiercest dog
went along together
looking for the ogres' island.

Momotaro Defeats the Ogres

At last they came to a wide river.
In the middle of the river was the island
of the ogres.
'I can help you cross the water,'
said the pheasant as Momotaro stood
looking at the waves of the river.
'Climb upon my back and we will fly across.'
'I will swim and carry monkey on my back,'
cried the fierce dog, and soon the friends came
to the ogres' island.
'How can we get into the castle?' said Momotaro.
'That is easy!' said the monkey and he scrambled
over the wall and turned the key in the lock
of the castle door.
The ogres were very surprised when the monkey
tripped them up, the fierce dog bit their ankles,
and the pheasant pecked their noses.
Momotaro soon had them under control
and the ogres promised never to steal
the people's cattle and treasure again.

Momotaro and his three friends returned to his village.
The old man and the old woman
and all the people in the village said,
'Momotaro is the bravest boy in all the world.'

Momotaro said, 'Without Monkey, Dog, and Pheasant,
I could not have beaten those ogres.
I am so glad that you made me
those millet flour dumplings!'

Can you make up music for Momotaro's river crossing?
What instrument might make the sound of flying?
Think how to make sounds for the rippling water,
the flapping pheasant, the scurrying monkey.
Ogres take huge steps when they walk.
Can you make a melody with wide leaps
to picture them?
How will you show the sounds of battle?
How will you show the ogres
tripping and falling?

A Song from Japan

Momotaro had animal friends.
Here is a Japanese song Momotaro
might have sung.
It is about feeding pigeons.
Do you see that there are only
five different notes in the song?
They are F, G, A, C, and D.
Many Japanese songs use only five notes.

Hato Popo

Folk Song from Japan   English Words by Jeffrey Yamashita

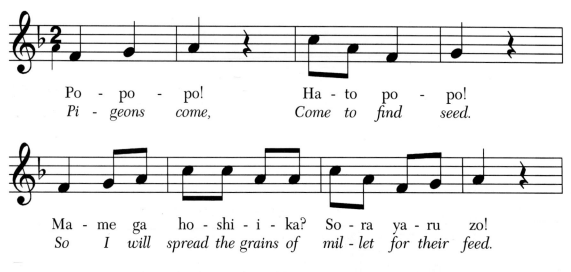

Po - po - po!   Ha - to po - po!
Pi - geons   come,   Come to find   seed.

Ma - me ga   ho - shi - i - ka? So - ra ya - ru   zo!
So   I   will   spread the grains of   mil - let for their feed.

Mi - na - de na - ka - yo - ku, Ta - be - ni   ko - i.
Come, love - ly pi - geons, take the mil - let for your need.

You can use the black keys of the piano, organ, or the black chime bars, as a five-note scale. Those five notes are G♭, A♭, B♭, D♭, and E♭.

Here is a black-key melody composed by David Stoner, a schoolboy of about your age. His sister, Amy, wrote it down.

In the photograph you can see David and Amy working at the keyboard.

Simple and Easy

David S. Stoner and Amy L. Stoner

Listen to the way an arranger has developed the Stoners' five-note melody.

Can you provide harmonies for the Stoners' melody using G♭, A♭, B♭, D♭, and E♭?

8 Simple and Easy . . . Stoner and Stoner

The Story of Divali

A Story from India

Prince Rama wanted to marry Sita, a beautiful princess.
Sita's father said, 'Only a prince
who is very strong can marry my daughter.
If you can bend this bow,
which is too heavy for men to use,
I shall believe that you are strong enough.'
So Rama picked up the great bow
and pulled on the bow-string.
The bow began to bend in Rama's grasp
and it bent so far that it snapped in half.
Sita's father was very impressed by Rama's strength
and Sita was delighted. 'You are certainly strong enough
to marry my daughter,' said Sita's father.
So Rama and Sita were married.

Rama was strong and brave.
He knew he could bend the bow.
Can you make a song for Rama?

You can make a melody for Rama
with these notes.

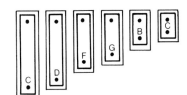

Use these two notes to go along
with Rama's melody.

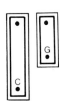

Make a dancelike melody for Sita.
Use these notes.

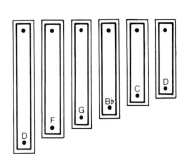

Use these notes to go along
with Sita's melody.

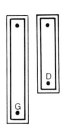

Do you know what sorts of instruments
people play in India?
Listen to the sound of a sitar.

Raga Yaman . . . . Traditional

More About Divali

When Rama's father became old, he wished that Rama
should become king in his place.
But the Queen wanted Rama's brother Bharata to be king
and she insisted that Rama and Sita be sent away.
The king reluctantly agreed, and Rama and Sita
went off to live in the forest
for fourteen years.

There they had many adventures.

One day, while Rama was away hunting,
a wicked demon called Ravana found Sita.
He carried her away in his ten arms
and locked her away in his castle.
Rama searched everywhere for Sita
but he could not find her.

At last the king of the monkeys, Hanuman,
came to Rama and told him
that he had seen Ravana,
the demon with ten heads and ten arms,
carry Sita away.

Hanuman called all his monkey people to him
and with their help Rama came to Ravana's castle
and rescued Sita.

By this time, King Bharata called on Rama
to replace him as king.
Rama and Sita returned to the city
riding on an elephant.
The journey was long and night began to fall
before they reached the city walls.
There was no moon that night
and it was very dark.
To guide them home to their city,
all the people put little lights,
or divas, outside their houses.
It looked so pretty that some people wondered
if the stars had fallen from the sky.

So Rama and Sita came home at last,
and to remember their great King Rama,
his people still light little lamps
and set off fireworks
to celebrate the time known as Divali,
or the time of lights.

Monkey Music

Perhaps Hanuman and his people
made their own monkey music.
What would such music sound like?
Try making some monkey music for Hanuman.
First, keep a steady beat on a drum.

Then, repeat this pattern several times over.

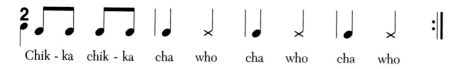

Chik - ka chik - ka cha who cha who cha who

Next, add this pattern.

Chit who chit - ta chat, chit - ta chat, chit who

Finally, this pattern will complete the chant.

Who chik - ka who chat - ta who chik - ka who chat - ta

Now you have three patterns.
Can you make up two more patterns to go
with the others?
What monkey-like word could you use?

Try forming five teams.
Each team can take one pattern.
Two teams will use the patterns
they have made up.
When all the patterns are performed at once,
you should hear some monkey-like sounds.
Listen to the recording to hear how
the first three patterns all go together.
Then add the other two patterns that you
have made up.

 **Monkey Music**

Glossary

ABA form (p. 120) A musical plan that has three parts, or sections. The first and last sections are the same. The middle section is different. 'Shoo, Fly' (p. 134) is a song in **ABA form**.

beat (p. 64) A repeating pulse that can be felt in some music. Pat the **beat** in your lap when you sing 'One, Two, Three, Alary' (p. 64).

crotchet (p. 93)— ♩ —Also called *quarter note*. *See* **note**.

downwards (p. 90) Moving from a higher tone to a lower one. 'Kite Song' ends with tones that move **downwards**.

even (p. 101) *See* **rhythm pattern**.

fast (p. 60) Moving quickly. The Ball (p. 65) is an example of music that is **fast**.

high (p. 60) A sound notated near the top of the stave. 'Do-Re-Mi' (p. 82) ends with a **high** sound.

introduction (p. 79) In a song, music played before the singing begins. Most songs on the music recordings begin with an instrumental **introduction**.

leap (p. 5) Moving from one note to another, skipping over the notes in between. 'It's Me!' (p. 4) begins with notes that **leap**.

long (p. 60) A sound that is not as short as others around it. 'The Lobster Quadrille' (p. 194) begins with two **long** sounds.

loud (p. 60) Not quiet. The music of Invocation of the Powerful Spirits (p. 143) is too **loud** to be a lullaby.

low (p. 60) A sound notated near the bottom of the stave. The verse of 'Growing-Up Song' (p. 48) begins with **low** notes.

lullaby (p. 108) A quiet song, often sung when rocking a child to sleep. 'Khasi's Lullaby' (p. 50) is a **lullaby**.

melody (p. 103) A line of single notes that move upwards, downwards, or repeat. The **melody** of 'Old Dan Tucker' (p. 116) begins with tones that repeat.

minim (p. 93)— ♩ —Also called *half note*. *See* **note**.

mood (p. 143) The feeling that a piece of music gives. The **mood** of 'Lullaby, My Jamie' (p. 142) is quiet and gentle.

no beat (p. 67) Giving no feeling of a repeated pulse. Listen for the sections with **no beat** in Moon Music (p. 67)

232 **Reference Bank**

note (p. 79) A symbol for sound in music. You have learned about quavers (♫), the crotchet (♩), and the minim (♩), also called *eighth notes, quarter note,* and *half note.*

phrase (p. 90) A musical 'sentence' that expresses one musical thought. There are five **phrases** in 'Who Has Seen the Wind?' (p. 106)

quavers (p. 93)— ♫ —Also called *eighth notes. See* **note.**

repeated notes (p. 84) Two or more notes in a row that have the same sound. 'Chumbara' (p. 88) begins with **repeated tones.**

rhythm pattern (p. 101) A grouping of long and short sounds. Some **rhythm patterns** have even sounds—

♩   ♫   ♩   ♩
long short short long   long

Other **rhythm patterns** have uneven sounds—

♩   ♪♩   ♪
long short long   short

score (p. 102) The printed music for a song or instrumental work. Follow the **score** on page 30 when you sing 'Who Built the Ark?'

section (p. 112) A part of a song or instrumental work. 'Scrapin' Up Sand' (p. 113) has two **sections,** A and B.

short (p. 60) A sound that is not as long as others around it. In Polka (p. 102) the xylophone melody has **short** sounds.

slow (p. 60) Not quick. In The Swan (p. 107) the cello plays a **slow** melody.

soft (p. 60) Quiet. We sing lullabies in a **soft** voice.

steady beat (p. 11) Regular pulses. Pat your lap to the **steady beat** when you sing your favourite song.

step (p. 84) Moving from one tone to another without skipping tones between. The verse of 'Do-Re-Mi' (p. 82) ends with notes that **step** upwards.

story song (p. 28) A song in which the words tell a story. 'Puff, the Magic Dragon' (p. 28) is a **story song.**

string instrument (p. 72) A musical instrument played by bowing, plucking, or strumming a string. A violin is a **string instrument.**

uneven (p. 101) *See* **rhythm pattern.**

up, upwards (p. 14) Moving from a lower tone to a higher one. 'There Was a Little Woman' (p. 86) begins with notes that move **upwards.**

Classified Index

FOLK AND TRADITIONAL SONGS

Africa
A-tin-go-tin   198
Go Well and Safely   146
Jog Trot, The   37
Kawakayima   200
Kee-Chee   70
Strength of the Lion, The   39

American Indian
Sunset   156

Austria
Star Song   53

Basque
At the Gate of Heav'n   108

Black America
Get on Board   118
Michael, Row the Boat Ashore   91
Run, Children, Run   152
Same Train   40
Shake Hands, Mary   90
Who Built the Ark?   30

Brazil
Cat, The   110

British Isles
Aiken Drum   100
Bravo   7
Court of King Caractacus, The   22
Gallant Ship, The   18
Haul Away, Joe   10
Lobster Quadrille, The   194
My Ship Sailed from China   188
Oats and Beans   12
Oranges and Lemons   16
Old John Braddelum   160
Romans and British   20
There Was a Little Woman   86
Today Is Monday   9

Canada
Chumbara   88

China
Temple Bell   164

Czechoslovakia
River, The   211

France
Are You Sleeping?   80
At the Gate of Heav'n   108

Germany
Ach ja!   145
Butzemann, The   104
My Hat   137

India
Khasi's Lullaby   50

Israel
From a Lovely Root   172
How Good and Joyous   163

Italy
Goat Song   158
Market Song   168
Ninna-nanna   109

Japan
Hato Popo   224
Rabbit   66
Teru Teru Bozu   219

Latvia
Lullaby, My Jamie   142

Mexico
Counting Song   46

Puerto Rico
El florón   144
Flower, The   144

Russia
Puppet Dance 186

Trinidad and Tobago
Growing-Up Song 48

United States
Big Corral, The 140
Built My Lady a Fine Brick
  House 112
Clear the Kitchen 94
Come and Dance 114
Jubilee! 148
Mister Sun 96
My Father's House 154
Old Dan Tucker 116
Polly Wolly Doodle 98
Rock About My Saro Jane 76
Rocky Mountain 84
Sandy Land 78
Scrapin' Up Sand 113
She'll Be Comin' Round the
  Mountain 170
Shoo, Fly 134
We're Going Round the Mountain
  68

LISTENING LIBRARY

Anonymous: Staines Morris Dance
  (excerpt) 161
Arnold: 'Grazioso' from English
  Dances 81
Beethoven: Minuet in G 120
Bizet: 'The Ball' from Children's
  Games 65
Chinese: High Moon 165
Coates: The Three Bears Fantasy
  32
Copland: 'Circus Music' from The
  Red Pony 25

Cowell: The Banshee 198
Debussy: 'The Snow Is Dancing'
  from Children's Corner Suite 166
Ginastera: 'Invocation of the
  Powerful Spirits' from
  Panambé 143
Knussen: 'First Interlude' from
  Where the Wild Things Are 45
Langford: Fanfare and Ceremonial
  Prelude 43
Mussorgsky: 'Ballet of the
  Unhatched Chicks' from Pictures
  at an Exhibition 93
Pinto: 'Run, Run' from Memories of
  Childhood 153
Ravel: 'Love for Two Cats' from
  L'Enfant et les sortilèges 111
Saint-Saëns: 'The Swan' from
  Carnival of the Animals 107
Shostakovich: 'Polka' from The
  Golden Age 102
Sousa: The Stars and Stripes
  Forever (excerpt) 177
Stoner and Stoner: Simple and
  Easy 225
Susato: Ronde 150
Susato: Saltarello 151
Villa-Lobos: 'The Little Train of the
  Caipira' from Bachianas
  Brasileiras No. 2 41
Walton: 'Tango Pasodoble' from
  Façade 44
Williams: Moon Music 67
Wood: 'Hornpipe' from Fantasia on
  British Sea Songs 11

POEMS

Lullaby, Oh, Lullaby! 51
This Happy Day 97
Who Has Seen the Wind? 106

Song Index

Ach ja! 145
Aiken Drum 100
Are You Sleeping? 80
At the Gate of Heav'n 108
A-tin-go-tin 198

Big Corral, The 140
Bongo Joe 6
Bravo 7
Built My Lady a Fine Brick
 House 112
Butzemann, The 104

Cat, The 110
Chitty Chitty Bang
 Bang 202
Chumbara 88
Circus Parade 24
Clear the Kitchen 94
Come and Dance 114
Cookie Jar (chant) 138
Counting Song 46
Court of King Caractacus,
 The 22

Do-Re-Mi 82

El florón 144
Every Mornin' 174

Flower, The 144

From a Lovely Root 172

Gallant Ship, The 18
Get on Board 118
Go Well and Safely 146
Goat Song 158
Growing-Up Song 48

Haul Away, Joe 10
Hato Popo 224
How Good and Joyous 163

In the Barnyard 92
It's Me! 4

Jog Trot, The 37
Jubilee! 148

Kawakayima 200
Kee-Chee 70
Khasi's Lullaby 50
Kite Song 14

Lazy John 101
Lobster Quadrille, The 194
Lullaby, My Jamie 142

Market Song 168
Michael, Row the Boat
 Ashore 91

Mission Control 54
Mister Sun 96
My Father's House 154
My Hat 137
My Ship Sailed from
   China 188

Nellie the Elephant 26
Ninna-nanna 109

Oh, I Do Like to Be Beside
   the Seaside 42
Oats and Beans 12
Old Dan Tucker 116
Old John Braddelum 160
One, Two, Three, Alary 64
Oranges and Lemons 16

Peanut Butter 162
Polly Wolly Doodle 98
Puff, the Magic Dragon 28
Puppet Dance 186

Rabbit 66
Race You Down the
   Mountain 69
River, The 211
Rock About My Saro
   Jane 76
Romans and British 20

Same Train 40
Sandy Land 78
Scrapin' Up Sand 113
Shake Hands, Mary 90
She'll Be Comin' Round the
   Mountain 170
Shoo, Fly 134
Sing a Rainbow 52
Star Song 53
Strength of the Lion, The 39
Sunset 156

Temple Bell 164
Teru Teru Bozu 219
There Was a Little
   Woman 86
Today Is Monday 9

Very Best Band, The 177

Waddaly Atcha 62
We're Going Round the
   Mountain 68
Who Built the Ark? 30
Who Has Seen the
   Wind? 106

Acknowledgments

Credit and appreciation are due the publisher and the copyright owners for use of the following.

'This Happy Day' from *The Little Hill,* Poems and Pictures by Harry Behn. Copyright 1949 by Harry Behn, copyright renewed © 1977 by Alice L. Behn. Used by permission of Marian Reiner.

'The Falling Star,' Reprinted with permission of Macmillan Publishing Company from COLLECTED POEMS by Sara Teasdale. Copyright 1930 by Sara Teasdale Filsinger, renewed 1958 by Guaranty Trust Company of New York.

Lilian Moore, 'Wind Song' from *I Feel The Same Way.* Text Copyright © 1967 Lilian Moore. Reprinted with the permission of Atheneum Publishers, Inc.

Picture Credits

Contributing Artists: Katherine Ace, George Bacquero, Mary Bausman, Rusty Coelho, Eulala Conner, Ed D'Agosta, Laurie Jordan, Christa Kieffer, Barbara Lanza, Richard Loehle, Michele Noiset, Tim O'Brien, Andrea Vuocolo, S. Michelle Wiggins, David Wisniewski.

Photographs: 2–3: background Don Rutledge/Tom Stack & Associates. 2: Bob Daemmrich. 3: © Robert Hagan/Focus West. 4: Silver Burdett & Ginn. 5: All photographs by Silver Burdett & Ginn except *b.l.* David Stone/Berg & Associates. 6–7: Silver Burdett & Ginn. 11: *t.* © Robert Hagan/Focus West; *b.* North Winds Picture Archives. 13: Silver Burdett & Ginn. 17: John Freeman & Co./Fotomas; inset Silver Burdett & Ginn. 19: *t.* Master & Fellows, Magdalene College, Cambridge; *l., r.* © Mary Rose Trust. 20–21: Silver Burdett & Ginn. 37: Animals Animals/© Zig Leszcynski. 42: Barry Hicks/Britain on View. 47: *l.* © Helen Marcus/Photo Researchers, Inc.; *t.r.* Allan A. Philiba; *b.r.* © Marta Sentis/Photo Researchers, Inc. 48: William Berssenbrugge/Shostal Associates. 49: M. Timothy O'Keefe/Bruce Coleman. 55: *t.* NASA. 61: Tina Mucci for Silver Burdett & Ginn. 63, 65, 67 & 71: Silver Burdett & Ginn. 72: *l.* J. Gerard Smith; *r.* Susan Johns. 73: *t.* Michal Heron; *l.* H. Oizinger/Leo deWys, Inc.; *r.* Susan Johns. 74–76: Silver Burdett & Ginn. 77: Paul Kuhn/Tom Stack & Associates. 80–81: Harald Sund. 83: Silver Burdett & Ginn. 84: Harald Sund. 88: Victoria Beller-Smith. 89: *t.l.* © 1988 Robert Frerck/Woodfin Camp & Associates; *m.* Harald Sund; *b.r.* R. Schmiedt/Leo deWys; *b.l.* Dan De Wilde. 93, 107: Silver Burdett & Ginn. 112: Silver Burdett & Ginn. 132–133: background Ron Krager/Tom Stack & Associates; inset Britain on View. 132: Sonia Halliday and Laura Lushington. 133, 136, 139, 143, 146, 147 & 149: Silver Burdett & Ginn. 151: New York Public Library Dance Collection, Cia Fornaroli Collection. 176: Dan De Wilde for Silver Burdett & Ginn. 180–181: background Ron Planck/Tom Stack & Associates. 180: *t., m.* Silver Burdett & Ginn; *b.* Dan De Wilde for Silver Burdett & Ginn. 181: *t.* Culver Pictures; *b.* Photo Trends. 187: © Reg Wilson Photography. 190: Lewis Carroll, *Alice's Adventures in Wonderland* and *Through the Looking-Glass,* J.M. Dent & Sons LTD, Publisher. 191: *Alice's Adventures in Wonderland* and *Through the Looking-Glass,* by Lewis Carroll. 192: Silver Burdett & Ginn. 193–195: *Alice's Adventures in Wonderland* and *Through the Looking-Glass,* by Lewis Carroll. 196: Wardene Weisser/Berg & Associates. 199: Silver Burdett & Ginn. 201: *t.* © George Holton/Photo Researchers, Inc.; *m.* © Stephen J. Krasemann/Peter Arnold, Inc.; *b.* Nadine Orabona/Berg & Associates. 204: E.R. Degginger. 205: *l.* J. Ballantyne/Leo deWys, Inc.; *r.* L. Davey/Leo deWys, Inc.; *b.* © Paul Barton/The Stock Market of NY. 206: *The Wind in the Willows,* by Kenneth Grahame, illustration by Ernest H. Shepard. 208: Silver Burdett & Ginn. 210: *The Wind in the Willows,* by Kenneth Grahame, illustration by Ernest H. Shepard. 212, 213, 225, 226 & 231: Silver Burdett & Ginn.